Fidelio

BLACK DOG OPERA LIBRARY

Fidelio

LUDWIG VAN BEETHOVEN
TEXT BY ROBERT LEVINE

BLACK DOG
& LEVENTHAL
PUBLISHERS
NEW YORK

Published by
Black Dog & Leventhal Publishers, Inc.
151 West 19th Street
New York, NY 10011

Distributed by
Workman Publishing Company
708 Broadway
New York, NY 10003

Designed by Alleycat Design, Inc.

Book manufactured in Singapore
ISBN: 1-57912-238-8

h g f e d c b a

FOREWORD

*B*eethoven, one of the greatest composers in Western history, composed just a single opera: *Fidelio.* Although it is alone in his body of work, *Fidelio* has joined the ranks of the world's great operas. It captures the essence of marital devotion, heroism in the face of dire consequences and the brutality of political tyranny—all in the simple story of Leonore and her quest to save her husband from a wrongful death behind bars. The story is timeless and the thrilling music Beethoven brings to it makes for a truly magnificent opera.

You will hear the entire opera in the two compact discs included on the inside front and back covers of this book. As you explore the book, you will discover the story behind the opera and its creation, the background of the composer, biographies of the principal singers and conductor, and the opera's text, or libretto, both in the original German and in an English translation. Special commentary has been included throughout the libretto to aid in your appreciation and to highlight key moments in the action and the score.

Enjoy this book and enjoy the music.

ABOUT THE AUTHOR

Robert Levine is a New York based travel and music writer. He was founding co-editor of Tower Records' *Classical Pulse!* magazine, helped launch amazon.com's classical music department, and has been editor-in-chief of andante.com. He is now senior editor at classicstoday.com. He is the author of *The Story of the Orchestra*, and the Black Dog Opera Library's volumes on Verdi's *Il trovatore* and Mozart's *Le nozze di Figaro.*

ACKNOWLEDGMENTS

Thanks to Paul Harrington for his hard work and research in preparing the manuscript.

PORTRAIT OF
LUDWIG VAN BEETHOVEN
BY JOSEF KARL STIELER

Fidelio

Ludwig van Beethoven is the indisputable demigod of classical music. No other composer's work has had the far-ranging effects of his, but unlike most of his contemporaries, he only wrote a single opera, *Fidelio,* and it was hardly performed more than a dozen times in its various versions during his lifetime.

Given the significance of his contribution to classical music, it should be no surprise then that his only opera has come to be so dramatically revered and often misinterpreted. A work created in an age of great change and the rise of the Romantic Movement, it generally became popular at times of political and social tumult. To take just one example, in Graz, Germany it was staged in 1933 as a pro-Nazi demonstration, in 1945 as a gesture to celebrate the fall of the Nazi government, and in 1956 to celebrate the city's post-war reconstruction. That an opera can be used for such diverse and even contrary events and purposes in the same city indicates its compelling complexity as well as its significance. Only a work of great import can be both used and misused with such potency. Furthermore, it is one of the staples of the operatic repertory, and no opera company of any significance goes for very long without a production of *Fidelio*.

How was it that in the early 19th century when opera was seen as the most significant art form in Vienna, which was not only the capital of the Austrian Empire, but also the very capital of European music, one of the greatest composers of classical music created only a single opera? To begin with we need to look back over his life and see how his philosophical and intellectual interests corresponded with his musical growth and the politics of Europe in the period. Ludwig van Beethoven was born in Bonn, Germany, in 1770. His father was a singer who recognized Ludwig's talents and sought to create another Mozart out of his son. Such demands made for a harsh childhood, and to further intensify this, Father Beethoven's alcoholism meant that Ludwig would have to take his place at the head of the family during his teenage years after his mother's unexpected death.

Although his father had been an oppressive martinet in his efforts to create in young Ludwig another Mozart, the young man still loved music. So great was this love that despite the brutality of his father's attempts to re-create Mozart in him, he would actually study under that great Master for a short time in Vienna in 1787. (It should be noted, however ironically, that Beethoven later claimed he learned little from Mozart, and never appreciated any reference to him in relation to his own work.) When his mother died he was forced to return to Bonn, and it was three years before he was able to go back to Vienna. Upon his return he studied under Haydn and Salieri, among other important composers of the period. He became known as a virtuoso pianist and was famous for his improvisational ability; no one could so brilliantly express and develop an original idea on the spur of the moment.

A decade after first coming to Vienna, Beethoven's career was booming. Sadly, it was about this time that he first noticed a problem that would have a dramatic effect upon his life: he was going deaf. By 1802 it was clear that medical treatments were useless, and he finally confronted the fact that he would eventually lose his hearing completely. In a letter written to his brothers, which he never actually mailed, he poignantly explained why he had never told them about his condition, and described how desperate he was. He wrote that the only thing keeping him from suicide was his art.

Luckily for the history of Western music his art did indeed keep him going, and in 1803 Beethoven was appointed to the post of composer for the Theater-an-der-Wien. Oddly, at this time there was something of a dearth of opera in Vienna. Part of the reason was that influential composers had changed their focus: Salieri had moved onto sacred music, which consumed the rest of his career, and others, such as Mozart's student Franz Xaver Süssmayr, had died. While Beethoven had not yet composed an opera he had written oratorios, such as *Christus am Oelberg,* Christ on the Mount of Olives), and contributed arias for others' works. It is likely that he was given the important job of composer at the Theater-an-der-Wien in an attempt to bring a breath of fresh German air to Viennese opera.

Beethoven's German-ness was an important factor because in the operatic drought that Vienna found itself the first effort to liven things up had come from the Court Theater, which had hired the Italian composer Luigi Cherubini from Paris in 1802. Cherubini would become very well known in time for his "rescue operas," in which the typical plot involved a hero or heroine being rescued by a

lover, spouse, or other agent. It was the use of spoken dialogue and "common" plot lines (one did not necessarily need an education to understand characters or story) in rescue opera that made it possible for political and social sentiments to come across clearly. In other words, unlike the earlier *tragedie lyrique* style, rescue operas were not associated with mythology, ancient Rome, or royal or aristocratic courts, and the ease with which they could communicate ideas made them ideal for use by Republicans as propaganda tools. While Cherubini's rescue operas invigorated opera in the city, their French-ness (and/or Italian-ness) rankled Vienna at a time when nationalism was beginning to take all of Europe by storm. Composer Johann Gottlieb Naumann said at the time, "I and all patriots wish that a good German operatic theater existed," and this was played out in the rivalry between the Theater-an-der-Wien and the Court Theater.

The first libretto Beethoven approached was *Vestas Feurer* by Emanuel Schikaneder, who was the author of Mozart's *The Magic*

Flute. He worked for a year on its composition, but he finally gave it up saying that it contained "language and verses such as could proceed only out of the mouths of our Viennese apple-women." It is well known that unlike Mozart, Beethoven never composed anything without a great deal of internal struggle. His original sheet music is awash in entire bars of music scratched out, ink blotches and other signs of the intense effort that went into each score. However, it is doubtful that it was only his inability to come to terms creatively with Schikaneder's libretto that caused him to stop work on *Vestas Feurer.*

Beethoven's generation had seen the American and French Revolutions and the rise of Napoleon Bonaparte, all of which influenced the mounting nationalism across Europe. The rational, reasoned music of Haydn and Mozart had suited its orderly times, but in the early 19th-century the passions that gave rise to the first successful popular political movements had begun to seep into the larger culture. This was the era, after all, of Byron and Shelley and Delacroix and Goya. Musicians responded to the emotionalism in literature and art, which rebelled against the settled, even sublimated, effects of the Classical era. The resulting Romanticism was the spirit of revolution, the people versus the Court.

Beethoven was an outspoken proponent of the French Revolution just as many German artists were. At the same time as he was working on his opera he was writing his magnificent third Symphony. This work was intended to be a tribute to Napoleon, but Beethoven rededicated it in disgust upon hearing that Bonaparte had crowned himself Emperor. Now called the *Eroica,* this symphony celebrates the heroic spirit of those who tore off the chains of tyranny. Clearly, whatever opera he would compose needed to be more concerned with this new ideology than one based, as *Vestas Feurer* was, in Imperial Rome.

Thus it is easy to see that Vienna's dislike of "French" operas was complicated by an admiration for the politics that had influenced these new works.
Indeed, while the Theater-an-der-Wien hired Beethoven to challenge the Court

SET SKETCH FOR A 1933 PRODUCTION OF FIDELIO IN GRAZ, GERMANY

Theater's Cherubini, Beethoven himself was quite impressed by the Italian composer and seems to have been looking in his direction when he began seeking a new libretto. Cherubini's popular *Les deux journees* had a text by Jean-Nicholas Bouilly, who was a favorite librettist of Beethoven's. Around this time Beethoven discovered what he called an "old French libretto" titled *Leonore, ou L'amour congugal,* which had been used in 1798 for an *opera comique* (a genre of French Opera circa 1790-1880 that contains spoken dialog and refers to any piece, whether serious or comic, that was not "through-composed," i.e. in which there were periods without music) of the same name by the French composer Pierre Gaveaux. This libretto had just the political significance that Beethoven was looking for.

Leonore was a tale said to be based on an actual event that had occurred in France during the Reign of Terror. In the town of Tours a woman had gained entry to the prison where her husband was illegally imprisoned by a political rival. Just as the prisoner was about to be killed his wife stepped forward with a pistol and shortly thereafter the trumpets announced the arrival of the Minister, who released the prisoner. As it turns out (and the story goes), Bouilly was actually the Minister in the event, and in order not to identify the people involved he moved the action of his libretto to 17th-century Spain. Nevertheless, it is easy to see how Beethoven would have been drawn to *Leonore.* The themes of freedom and loyalty (conjugal and otherwise) and tale of an individual's confrontation and defeat of a tyrant surely meshed with the political and philosophical ideas that were so important to him at the time when he was writing the *Eroica* symphony.

Once he discovered the story that would best fit his creative and philosophical needs, Beethoven set to work on a score, and Joseph Ferdinand Sonnleithner, who had replaced Schikaneder at the Theater-an-der-Wien, began work on the libretto. The characters that inhabit Sonnleithner's libretto range from the mundane to the dangerous to the noble. Leonore is the courageous, righteous woman who infiltrates the prison to save her husband, passing herself off as an apprentice jailer, Fidelio. As her husband, Florestan, represents political loyalty, she represents conjugal loyalty ("I follow a voice within me, unwavering, and am strengthened by the faith of wedded love." Act 1, no. 9). Rocco, the jailer, is a regular guy, somewhat of a bumpkin, who only wants to marry his daughter, Marzelline, to a good man and ensure her future. Towards that end he is willing to do whatever Don Pizarro, the governor of the prison, commands as long as he may avoid responsibility for the deed ("I do what my duty demands, but I hate all cruelty." Act 2, no. 13). Don Pizarro, however, is pure evil in the leering, mustache-twirling tradition. A canny and well-connected political operator, he is pleased to kill his enemy and prisoner, Florestan and remove a thorn from his own side ("To run him through the heart, what rapture, what great joy!" Act 1, no. 7). Florestan is simply a good, God-fearing man, who made an enemy out of Don Pizarro by opposing his tyranny. While he is awaiting release, he does not plot

revenge, rather he accepts his fate and dreams of rescue by his angelic wife ("O cruel trial! But God's will is just! I'll not complain!" Act 2, no. 11). While Leonore (as Fidelio) eventually stops Pizarro from killing Florestan, it is the arrival of the minister, Don Fernando, who represents good government, who puts an end to Pizarro's villainy and saves the reunited husband and wife ("No longer kneel like slaves before me, no cruel tyrant am I; a brother has come to seek his brothers, to help them, if he can, with all his heart." Act 2, no. 16). The final two and least complex of the characters are Marzelline, an innocent teenager, who unwittingly falls in love with Fidelio ("A wonderful feeling fills me and grips my very heart; he loves me, it is clear: oh how happy I shall be!" Act 1, no. 3), and Jaquino, the prison's gatekeeper, who is also quite young, but so taken with Marzelline that he is able to avoid the darkness of his job—and several of its responsibilities—by focusing on his unrequited love ("I was getting on so well, and now my prize escapes me again." Act 1, no. 1).

While these characters are certainly stereotypical, one cannot help but be struck by the multiplicity of meanings and feelings that are to be found in them and their words. The complexity of this tale and its musical treatment by Beethoven is stunningly illustrated just ten minutes into the action, in a quartet, "Mir ist so wunderbar," wherein Marzelline sings of her love for Fidelio; Leonore/Fidelio expresses her fear at the danger and near hopelessness of her mission and feels for Marzelline; Rocco acknowledges and approves of his daughter's love for Fidelio; and Jaquino realizes that he has no chance to win Marzelline now that even Rocco seems to be hoping that Fidelio will marry

FRIEDERICH SCHORR IN 1927
AS DON PIZARRO

25

Marzelline. Musically this piece is quite beautiful, but its greatness lies further in the masterful manner in which Beethoven manages to weave these four very distinct points of view with amazing clarity through music that does not merely work as background for the words, but actually adds even greater depth and detail to the words being sung. It is a moment frozen in time, and it tells us worlds about our characters and their situations early in the opera.

Given that Beethoven's *raison d'être* at the Theater-an-der-Wien was to create a more German opera, we might wonder why he turned to France for a libretto with which to do it. As we have seen, artists not only from Germany, but all across Europe were attempting to establish a national unity and identity. Beethoven did precisely what others were doing in his day, which was to turn to folk tales, folk songs and other native artistic elements to put their culture's indelible stamp on their art. In German literature the fairy tales collected by the Brothers Grimm best represent this, and in music it was the use of *Singspiel*—a down-to-earth German operatic style similar to opera comique that involved talking parts as well as sung ones, with melodies for the minor, lighter characters that were deceptively simple and "folksy"—that gave Beethoven and Sonnleithner a tool to create a specifically German opera.

Yet it is not only in operatic genre that *Fidelio* becomes more German. Indeed, it is Beethoven's music that completes the translation from "French" to "German." *Fidelio* is often called an opera in a symphonic style, and certainly Beethoven's emphasis on the orchestra as commentator rather than mere accompaniment is notable. But he also wrote the voice parts as if he were writing for instruments rather than human voices; and it is partially because each of the "noble" characters' parts is so difficult that this work manages to capture the intensity that he sought. In lighter moments such as those between Marzelline and Jaquino using easily melodic *Singspiel*-type melodies gives a German grounding to a work that was out of the French style. The music of Leonore, Florestan and Pizarro, however, is as complex and exclamatory as is called for by the characters' definitions. The passionate and emotional symphonic composition and challenging vocal parts imparted a signature that was quite nationally distinct at the time.

As we have seen, however, nothing that Beethoven did came without an effort equal in intensity to the music that resulted. As he and Sonnleithner were setting to work, Bouilly's libretto and Gaveaux's score had been published and this seems to have resulted in a bit of fame for the story. In Dresden, Italian composer Ferdinando Paer staged a version called *Leonora, ossia l'amore Congugal* in 1804. Paer's version was in Italian and while a copy of the score was found among Beethoven's possessions at the time of his death, it did not have as much influence as Gaveaux's apparently did on Beethoven, as echoes of Gaveaux's version

GABRIELA BENACKOVA AS LEONORE AND GARY LAKES AS FLORESTAN
IN A 1994 PRODUCTION AT THE NEW YORK'S METROPOLITAN OPERA

can be heard in his. (The best example of this is in Beethoven's treatment of the prisoners' chorus near the close of the opera's first act, with its long-held bass notes and gradual rise in pitch and volume as the men emerge from their cells

LUDWIG VON BEETHOVEN CONDUCTING RASUMOWSKY QUARTETTE

into the light of day after a long period of imprisonment.) Nevertheless, while he may have had examples of others' interpretations of Bouilly's story to influence his efforts, they did not seem to speed his work; it was not before the autumn of 1805 that his score was complete and the opera first performed.

This first performance was remarkable for many reasons, foremost among them being the fact that its intended audience was not present for it. Beethoven's fans—that is, the rich merchants and aristocrats, as well as Empress Josephine herself—who admired his complicated music (which was considered quite "new" at the time), had fled Vienna with the coming of Emperor Napoleon's army. Fifteen thousand French troops marched into the city just days before the premiere on November 20th. It is unlikely that Napoleon himself was even aware of the performance, and the Theater-an-der-Wien was not more than half-filled with an audience made up mostly of French soldiers who understood little German. Given the already immense effort he had put into composing his first opera in the prior two years, the French invasion was only the beginning of his frustrations. Among the others was the title that Beethoven wished to give the work, *Leonore.* To his consternation, the directors of the theater were concerned that the audience would confuse his version with the others

WILLARD WHITE IN
A 1993 PRODUCTION
OF FIDELIO AT LON-
DON'S ROYAL OPERA

already extant, and so advertised the opera as *Fidelio oder die ehiliche Liebe* (Fidelio or Conjugal Love).

Critical reaction was not much warmer than that of the audience. August von Kotzebue wrote in the literary journal, *Die Freimuthige,* that "the music was really way below the expectations of amateur and professional alike." He went on to say, "The melodies as well as the general character, much of which is affected, lack that happy, clear, magical impression of emotion which grips us so irresistibly in the works of Mozart and Cherubini. The music has some beautiful passages, but it is very far from being a perfect, yes, even successful work."

Meanwhile, *Allgemeine Musikalische Zeitung* rendered this verdict:

"Up to now Beethoven has sacrificed beauty so many times for the new and strange; thus this characteristic of newness and a certain originality in creative idea was expected from this first theatrical production of his—and it is exactly these qualities that are the least in evidence."

Interestingly, both of these critics agree that they disliked Beethoven's opera, but they seem to disagree on the reasons for its failure. The former says it lacked the "Classical" elements as well as those that one expected from the "French" operas of Cherubini, but the latter claims that Beethoven had failed to deliver the "newness" that the audience expected from his work. With this reaction it is not surprising that the opera closed after a few performances; however, this was not the end of the story: in early 1806 a group of Beethoven's patrons and friends gathered over dinner at Prince Lichnowsky's palace and induced, coaxed and prodded the composer into editing his work.

Unsurprisingly, this was no easy effort, but it did end with Beethoven severely altering the opera and his friend Stephen von Breuning reworking the libretto. The results reduced the three acts to two, an aria for Rocco was cut

A 1978
SAN FRANCISCO
OPERA

entirely and the "melodrama" (in this instance, quite different from what we have come to expect: an operatic melodrama is a scene in which spoken lines are accompanied or punctuated by music) in the Dungeon Scene abridged. Finally, Beethoven wrote a new overture—Leonore no. 3. (The first had never been performed and the second was not performed after the unsuccessful premiere.) On March 29th, 1806 the second version of the opera was performed, and this time *Allgemeine Musikalische Zeitung* said, "An entire act has been omitted, but the piece has benefited and pleased better."

Despite the critical reaction, the 1806 version was not seen more than the earlier one, because Beethoven chose to withdraw the score after a disagreement over fees with the theater. The years following his frustrations with his sole attempt at opera seem to have put Beethoven off any further involvement with theatrical music and he returned to other compositions. He was therefore taken by surprise when his friend the librettist Georg Friedrich Treitschke approached him in 1814 asking permission to revise the libretto of *Fidelio* and set about persuading the composer to produce yet another version of the score. In his response he wrote to Treitschke, "I could compose something new much more quickly than patching up the old. . . . I have to think out the whole work again . . . this opera will win me a martyr's crown."

An old expression has it that the third time is the charm, and this seems to have been the case with *Fidelio*. Beethoven told his biographer, Anton Schinder, "Of all the children of my spirit, this one is the dearest to me, because it was the most difficult to bring into the world." While it may have won him a "martyr's crown" and probably because it was "dearest" to him of all his works, it has also become considered one of his most significant works. The themes of loyalty and of struggle against tyranny, which as general concepts are quite easy

to apply to any given situation (as they have been in Graz), are as relevant today as they were in the early 19th-century. *Fidelio,* like his Ninth Symphony, which incorporates Schiller's idealistic Ode to Joy, has come to remind us not only of Beethoven's greatness, but of the complicated, vital nature of the important ideas that his music represents.

LOTTE LEHMANN AND LUISE
HELLETSGRUBER AS LEONORE AND
MARZELLINE IN SALZBURG, AUSTRIA

The Story of Fidelio

ACT 1

Fidelio takes place at a prison in Seville, Spain. We find ourselves in the court-yard of the home of Rocco, who is the jailer of the prison. Rocco's daughter, Marzelline, is doing her best to avoid the affections of his assistant, Jaquino. The young man pitches his woo insistently without any encouragement whatsoever from the girl, and under considerable difficulties resulting from his job. While Marzelline herself is attempting to focus on her ironing, rather than on Jaquino, the poor fellow is repeatedly interrupted in mid-pitch by those who come to the door that he is supposed to be attending. Nevertheless, he does manage to pro-pose to her (Jetzt, Schatzchen, jetzt sind wir allein/Now my treasure, now we are alone). When he is finally called away and cannot immediately return, Marzelline breathes a sigh of relief and reveals that while she feels badly for Jaquino, she actually loves another of her father's assistants, Fidelio (O war ich schon mit dir vereint/Oh, were we only married now). What she does not know is that Fidelio is actually a woman, Leonore, in disguise, who has insinuated her-self into the prison in an effort to find her husband, Florestan, whom she believes is being secretly held here by the villainous prison governor, Pizarro. Fidelio has been on the job for six months and while she has yet to find Florestan, she has

INTERIOR OF THE
OPERA HOUSE IN
GRAZ, GERMANY

1994 METROPOLITAN OPERA PRODUCTION OF FIDELIO

gained the affection and devotion of both Rocco and his daughter. Rocco enters, accompanied by Jaquino, saying that he is expecting Fidelio back from the city with some new chains. Fidelio arrives soon after and is congratulated by Rocco for acquiring a particularly sturdy set of chains at a very good price.

A quartet follows (Mir ist so wunderbar/It is so wonderful for me), sung as a canon (a musical form similar to a "round"), in which Marzelline shows that she thinks that Fidelio returns her affections; Leonore notes Marzelline's regard, feels badly about it and ruminates on how slim her "ray of hope" of finding her husband is; Rocco thinks they would make a fine couple; and Jaquino realizes that his cause might be lost. Rocco next promises that he will make Fidelio his son-in-law, once the governor leaves for Seville. Being a practical man, Rocco makes a point of reminding Fidelio in an aria that money is as important as love (Hat man nicht auch Gold beineben/If you have no money), and explains that one who has only love on the table goes away hungry. Fidelio agrees and in the ensuing dialogue learns that there is a prisoner kept so secret that no one besides Rocco is allowed to visit him.

Overjoyed to finally hear some indication that her suspicions were correct, Leonore suggests that she might be allowed to assist Rocco with his arduous duties deep in the dungeons. Leonore asks about this secret prisoner and Rocco says that the man has been there for two years, and that for the last two months he, Rocco, has been ordered to reduce his rations to only two ounces of black bread a day. Leonore/Fidelio declares that "he" has the strength to see the prisoner. Rocco approves "his" resolution (Gut, Sohnchen, gut/Good, my boy, good), not realizing that Leonore's/Fidelio's resolve comes from her love for her husband who has been missing for two years, and not from love for his daughter. Marzelline, however, understands Leonore's/Fidelio's words as kindness towards Rocco, and urges her father to permit his assistant to accompany him. Suddenly a march is heard and the main gate of the prison is opened for a troop of soldiers and governor Pizarro. The governor posts soldiers on the walls and gets his mail from Rocco. One of the letters turns out to be a warning about an upcoming surprise visit from the prime minister, Don Fernando, who has heard that Pizarro has been misusing his powers. Pizarro immediately thinks of Florestan: the minister believes him dead.

There is only one way to ensure that he never learns that Florestan is here, and Pizarro excitedly realizes that the time has come for revenge on this political enemy he has held secretly for so long (Ha! Welch ein Augenblick!/Ha! What a moment!). The soldiers note their commander's excitement and comment that the letter must be important; after all, he is talking about death. Pizarro calls his captain to him and orders him up into a tower with a trumpeter to warn of the first sign of an approaching coach with an escort.

He then turns to Rocco and promises the greedy jailer gold in return for his speedy assistance (Jetzt, Alter, jetzt hat es Eile!/Now, old man, we must hurry!) in dealing with the secret prisoner. The offer of money eases Rocco's discomfort with the situation—after all, he says, a quick death is probably better than the slow starvation he's been suffering—but he still makes it very clear that he will not kill anyone. Pizarro agrees to commit the murder himself and says that he only needs Rocco to deal with the body after the deed is done. Pizarro is in a frenzy of blood-lust as he and Rocco leave the courtyard to speak further in the garden.

Leonore, meanwhile, has been listening from a concealed spot, and as they leave she sings her great aria (Abscheulicher! Wo eilst du hin?/Monster! Where are you hurrying?), summoning her courage and calling upon Hope to help her in her duty as a loyal wife. Leonore then follows them into the garden. As she goes, Marzelline comes out of the house followed by Jaquino pleading with her to accept his proposal, but she finally tells him in no uncertain terms that she is not interested. Rocco and Fidelio join them and Rocco tells Jaquino that he has more important matters to deal with. Leonore suggests to Rocco that as the weather is so good, he should permit the prisoners from the upper cells out into the garden. He is unwilling to do so without Pizarro's permission, but Marzelline knows that, since her father and the governor were talking for so long in private, Rocco must be doing Pizarro a great favor. She thus suggests that he would not mind the jailer taking this liberty. Rocco tells his assistants to let the prisoners out and leaves to find Pizarro.

This release is a luxury rarely permitted to the prisoners and their chorus as they come into the sunlight and nervously eye the guards on the walls is transcendental in its joy and celebration of liberty (O welche Lust, in freier Luft/O what pleasure, in the open air). However, an officer on the wall sees the prisoners and goes off to tell Pizarro, and the prisoners talk softly amongst themselves treasuring their few minutes in the sun and fresh air.

Rocco returns from his interview with Pizarro and tells his assistant that he has received the governor's permission to marry Marzelline, but now they must dig the grave of the secret prisoner. Misunderstanding Leonore's (Fidelio's) horrified response as a reaction to the heavy work of digging a grave, he offers to let "him" off; however, once Leonore confirms that the prisoner has not yet been killed, she insists on helping him. Meanwhile, Pizarro, having heard of the unauthorized liberty accorded the prisoners, returns angrily. Rocco mollifies him saying aloud that it is the King's name day, and more quietly, reminding him of the man to be killed below. Pizarro stops ranting, but the prisoners are returned to their cells as the act ends.

ACT 2

The second act begins in the dark gloom of Florestan's cell. Chained to a stone, he comments first on the darkness and then on the horrible two years of uninterrupted imprisonment he has suffered. In a moving aria (In des Lebens Fruhlingstagen/In the Springtime days of life) he remembers his happy life before imprisonment and imagines Leonore as an angel leading him up to heaven. Weakened and exhausted by his trials, he collapses.

Rocco and Leonore come down the stairs to dig the grave in the cell's cistern. The scene is technically called a "melodrama": that is, there is spoken dialogue above music from the orchestra. As they work, Leonore shudders in the cold and attempts to make out whether the unconscious prisoner is actually alive and whether it is actually Florestan. After some difficult work they take a break and Rocco offers the prisoner some wine.

Finally conscious, Florestan asks who the governor of the prison is and asks Rocco to get word to his wife, Leonore, in Seville that he is imprisoned. His identity confirmed, Leonore offers him some bread, and in a beautiful trio Florestan thanks her for her kindness (Euch werde Lohn in bessern Welten/You will be rewarded in a better world). Their work finished, Rocco whistles the agreed upon signal to Pizarro. Florestan, knowing Pizarro's nature, correctly fears that his life is near its end.

Pizarro comes down the stairs and gloatingly reveals his identity to Florestan who had attempted to overthrow him (Er sterbe! Doch er soll erst wissen/He shall die! Yet first let him know). Florestan prepares for his death with great dignity, but just as Pizarro draws his dagger and prepares to enact his revenge, Leonora cries, "First kill his wife!" and moves forward to intervene.

Each man confronts this revelation. Pizarro, surprised, decides to kill both of them, but in a second surprise move Leonore draws a pistol, which brings all action to a halt.

At that moment a trumpet sounds from off stage and Jaquino appears at the top of the stairs to announce the arrival of the minister. Suddenly the circumstances have changed dramatically: Florestan is saved and Pizarro is in immense trouble. Rocco orders Jaquino to come down into the dungeon with soldiers and escort Pizarro away.

Leonore and Florestan remain and sing of their happiness at their reunion (O namenlose Freude!/Oh nameless joy!).

We now move to the parade ground of the prison. Soldiers march in and the Minister Don Fernando appears along with Don Pizarro. The townspeople gather and Jaquino and Marzelline lead in the prisoners. All kneel before the minister and welcome him (Heil! Heil sei dem Tag!/Hail! Hail to the day!), and Don Fernando announces that he has come at the King's command and assures the crowd of the King's mercy and speaks about the brotherhood of men.

Then, Rocco pushes through the crowd leading Florestan and Leonore. Astonished to see Florestan, whom he thought dead, and Leonore dressed as a boy, Don Fernando has events explained to him. He has Pizarro dragged off for punishment and the people rejoice, and he tells Leonore to remove Florestan's chains. In the end, all sing in praise of Leonore and conjugal love (Wer ein holdes Weib errungen/He who has won a beloved wife) as the curtain drops to exultation.

The Performers

INGA NIELSEN   The Danish soprano Inga Nielsen studied in Vienna, Stuttgart and Budapest before beginning her career in Germany and Switzerland. She joined the Frankfurt Opera and went on to perform at major opera houses throughout the world, including the Vienna State Opera, La Scala, Milan and Covent Garden as well as the Bayreuth, Salzburg, Vienna, Munich, Aix-en-Provence and Edinburgh Festivals. These varied performances have led to appearances as a television and radio concert soloist and to several recordings. Her 1994 appearances as Salome in Leipzig and as the Marschallin in *Der Rosenkavalier* at the Royal Danish Opera were notable successes and her performances as the Empress in *Die Frau ohne Schatten* at La Scala, under the late Giuseppe Sinopoli and in a number of Wagnerian roles have continued to establish her formidable reputation. Queen Margarethe of Denmark noted Nielsen's cultural contributions by honoring her with the Order of the Dannebrog in 1992.

INGA NIELSEN PERFORMS IN A ROYAL OPERA PRODUCTION OF MATHIS DER MALER

KARITA MATTILA AND GOSTA WINBERGH PERFORM IN A ROYAL OPERA PRODUCTION OF
LOHENGRIN

GOSTA WINBERGH   Before making his debut in 1973 in Gothenburg, Gosta Winbergh studied at the Opera Conservatory in Stockholm. Soon after his debut he became a member of the Royal Opera in Stockholm, where his roles included Don Ottavio, Count Almaviva, Tamino, Nemorino and Rodolfo. He has been a member of the Zurich Opera, singing many Mozart roles in productions staged by Jean-Pierre Ponnelle and conducted by Nikolaus Harnoncourt; he also appears internationally in major opera houses and festivals. Recently Winbergh has taken on heavier roles and has succeeded brilliantly in several Wagner operas. These roles have included Walther in *Die Meistersinger* in Berlin and at Covent Garden, Erik in *The Flying Dutchman* in Venice and Lohengrin in many of the world's great opera houses. Along with his stage reputation, he has numerous recordings to his credit and is also highly regarded as a concert soloist and recitalist.

KURT MOLL   Now indisputably one of the world's great basses, Kurt Moll completed his studies at Cologne's Musikhochschule and his first appearances were at provincial opera houses in Aachen, Mainz and Wuppertal. He was signed to the Staatsoper in Hamburg in 1970, and in the same year made his debut at the Salzburg Festival as Sarastro in Mozart's *The Magic Flute.* Since then his career has taken him to La Scala, Covent Garden and New York's Metropolitan Opera and he is well known at the Bayreuth and Salzburg Festivals. Throughout his prestigious career he has made over 100 recordings and is in as great demand as a recitalist and concert singer as he is on the opera stage. Moll has also won several prizes, including the prestigious title of Kammersanger from three different opera houses. He has been a professor at the Cologne Musikhochschule since 1992.

EDITH LIENBACHER   Born in Karnten, Austria, Edith Lienbacher studied at the Conservatory in Klagenfurt and then studied with Hilde Rossl-Majdan at the Vienna Musikhochschule. After winning the Richard Tauber Competition in London she was engaged at the Vienna Volksoper and has been a member of the Vienna Staatsoper since 1989. Her repertoire there has included roles in Mozart operas and several operettas. She has also won acclaim for her performances at major international festivals and in the great opera houses of the world. This diverse singer is equally at home as a Lieder and concert singer and was honored in 1999 with the title Kammersangerin.

ALAN TITUS   Baritone Alan Titus was born in New York and studied at the Juilliard School. His debut was at the Washington Opera, and since then he has appeared at all of the leading opera houses in the United States and Europe. As a regular guest at the Munich State Opera he has won acclaim for his performances as Olivier in *Capriccio,* Guglielmo in *Cosi fan tutte* and as the eponymous heroes in *Le nozze di Figaro* and Hindemith's *Cardillac.* He debuted at La Scala, Milan as Mandryka in a new production of *Arabella.* Titus has won several awards including Singer of the Year from the magazine Opernwelt and the title Kammersanger from the Munich State Opera. He is known as a recitalist and concert singer and has made several recordings including *Le nozze di Figaro* and *Falstaff* with Sir Colin Davis and *Don Giovanni* with Rafael Kubelik.

THOMAS MOSER AS FLORESTAN AND WALTRAUD MEIER AS LEONORE AT MILAN'S LA SCALA IN 1999

WOLFGANG GLASHOF   Born in 1957, Wolfgang Glashof studied medicine before turning to singing at the Conservatory of Nuremberg. Debuting at the National Theatre in Mannheim, he has appeared at opera houses in Dusseldorf, Berlin and Vienna in roles such as Figaro in *Il barbiere di Siviglia* and Danilo in *Die lustige Witwe* and is also a concert soloist and recitalist throughout Europe.

HERWIG PECORARO   Herwig Pecoraro studied at the Conservatories in Vorarlberg and Modena and also took part in master classes with Elisabeth Schwarzkopf. His appearances throughout the world have included stops in Milan, Paris, Vienna and Los Angeles, as well as at the Salzburg and Bregenz Festivals. He has also appeared on television and radio and since 1991 has been a member of the Vienna Staatsoper.

HUNGARIAN RADIO CHORUS   Established in 1950 to perform unaccompanied and orchestral choral works, the Hungarian Radio Chorus has long established its reputation for excellence. During its existence the chorus has given performances of a number of works specially written for them and been invited to the Bayreuth, Edinburgh and Salzburg Festivals. Great conductors like Dorati, Masur and Menuhin have led the chorus and Solti conducted them in several very well received concerts with the Berlin Philharmonic Orchestra. Since its foundation the chorus has also made over 80 recordings.

NICOLAUS ESTERHAZY SINFONIA   Ibolya Toth of the Hungarian Phoenix Studio founded the Nicolaus Esterhazy Sinfonia in 1992 with members of the Hungarian

State Orchestra. The conductor of the Sinfonia is the flautist Bela Drahos and there are several excellent musicians, including the principal wind-players of the Symphony Orchestra, that have contributed to its stellar reputation.

MICHAEL HALASZ   After beginning his career as conductor at the Munich Gartnerplatz Theater, Michael Halasz moved to Frankfurt as Principal Conductor under Christoph von Dohnanyi. There he conducted all of the important works of the opera repertoire, and worked with some of the most distinguished singers. He was also guest conductor of the Deutsche Oper Berlin, State Opera Hamburg and in Turin. In 1977 he went to the Hamburg State Opera with Dohnanyi to be Principal Conductor there until 1978 when he became General Music Director of the Hagen Opera House. At the same time he conducted in the major opera houses of Germany. In 1991 he took up the post of Resident Conductor of the Vienna State Opera. Since that time he has appeared all over the world and since 1995 has been invited to conduct the ABC orchestras in Australia. Halasz has made over thirty recordings.

The

Libretto

A NOTE ABOUT THE OVERTURE

Through his various re-writes of the opera, Beethoven composed four overtures for *Fidelio*. The first one was used at its premiere in 1805, but is now known as Leonore No. 2. Leonore No. 3 was composed for the 1806 revision, and it was then simplified for a performance in Prague that never actually occurred. This manuscript was then lost until 1832; when it was found, it was assumed to be the first one Beethoven had composed. Therefore, it was mistitled Leonore No. 1. The fourth overture was written for the 1814 performance and is known as the Fidelio Overture. In its brief excitement Beethoven introduces the relatively light-hearted opening scene far more interestingly than in the early versions, and it is this overture that is used in modern productions.

Cast

LEONORE .... *Inga Nielsen*

FLORESTAN .... *Gosta Winbergh*

ROCCO .... *Kurt Moll*

DON PIZARRO .... *Alan Titus*

MARZELLINE .... *Edith Lienbacher*

JAQUINO .... *Herwig Pecoraro*

DON FERNANDO .... *Wolfgang Glashof*

CONDUCTOR: *Michael Halasz*

NICOLAUS ESTERHAZY SINFONIA

HUNGARIAN RADIO CHORUS

Act 1

OVERTURE

disc no.1/track 1 Unlike many other opera overtures, the Fidelio overture does not contain any themes from the opera. It is an attention-getting statement, with horns and winds very important to its texture. Within its brief six or seven minutes, Beethoven manages to work the audience into a frenzy of anticipation.

The Court Yard of a State Prison. In the background, the principal gate, and a high rampart wall, over which trees are seen branching out. In the gate, which is closed, there is a little door for foot-passengers. At the side of the gate is the gatekeepers lodge. The side scenes on the left present the dwelling of the prisoners. All the windows are grated; and the doors, which are marked with numbers, are strongly bolted. At the foremost wing, is the door of the residence of the Turnkey.

SCENE 1

MARZELLINE, JAQUINO
(Marzelline plättet vor ihrer Tür Wäsche, neben ihr steht ein Kohlenbecken, in dem sie den Stahl wärmt. Jaquino hält sich nahe bei seinem Stübchen, öffnet die Tür mehreren Personen, die ihm Packete übergeben, welche er in sein Stübchen legt.)

MARZELLINE, JAQUINO
(Marzelline is seen ironing linens at her door, near her stands the firepan in which she heats her irons. Jaquino, who keeps closer to the door, opens it to several persons, who present him with parcels or packets of letters: he carries them into his little room.)

Duett The first music we hear as the curtain rises is particularly surprising after the sheer weight of emotion with which the overture closes. In fact, its lightness seems to belong to another opera entirely. The early musical numbers—the opening duet and Marzelline's aria (and a bit later, Rocco's "gold" aria)—are simple, songlike structures with short, conversational vocal lines that represent ideally Rocco's working-class, simple family circle and circumstances. The situation may be mundane—Marzelline is ironing in the opening duet—but the feelings run deeper; Beethoven uses the old Singspiel, folksy structure, but he takes the form and runs with it.

JAQUINO *(verliebt und sich die Hände reibend)*
Jetzt, Schätzchen, jetzt sind wir allein, wir
können vertraulich nun plaudern.

MARZELLINE *(ihre Arbeit fortsetzend)*
Es wird ja nichts Wichtiges sein, ich darf
bei der Arbeit nicht zaudern.

JAQUINO
Ein Wörtchen, du Trotzige, du!

MARZELLINE
So sprich nur, ich höre ja zu.

JAQUINO
Wenn du mir nicht freundlicher blickest,
so bring' ich kein Wörtchen hervor.

MARZELLINE
Wenn du dich nicht in mich schickest, ver-
stopf' ich mir vollends das Ohr.

JAQUINO
Ein Weilchen nur höre mir zu, dann laß'
ich dich wieder in Ruh'.

JAQUINO
Now, my little treasure, we are alone, now
we may chat in confidence.

MARZELLINE
Surely it cannot be so important, I dare not
tarry at my work.

JAQUINO
Just a word, you cross one, you!

MARZELLINE
Well, speak; I'm all attention.

JAQUINO
If you look so cross, I won't say a word.

MARZELLINE
If you won't please me, I'll block my ears
altogether.

JAQUINO
One moment only—listen,

MARZELLINE
So hab' ich denn nimmermehr Ruh', so
rede, so rede nur zu.

JAQUINO
Ich habe zum Weib dich gewählt, ver-
stehst du?

MARZELLINE
Das ist ja doch klar.

JAQUINO
Und wenn mir dein Jawort nicht fehlet,
was meinst du?

MARZELLINE
So sind wir ein Paar.

JAQUINO
Wir könnten in wenigen Wochen –

MARZELLINE
Recht schön, du bestimmst schon die Zeit.
(Man pocht.)

JAQUINO
Zum Henker, das ewige Pochen! (für sich)
Da war ich so herrlich im Gang, und
immer entwischt mir der Fang!

MARZELLINE
So bin ich doch endlich befreit! (für sich)
Wie macht seine Liebe mir bang', wie werden die Stunden mir lang! (Jaquino öffnet
die Pforte, nimmt ein Packet ab, und legt es
ins Stübchen; unterdessen fährt Marzelline
fort.) Ich weiß, daß der Arme sich quälet,

MARZELLINE
Never more shall I rest.

JAQUINO
I will then leave you alone! I have chosen a
wife—do you know that it's you?

MARZELLINE
Surely that's plain enough.

JAQUINO
And if I got your consent, what mean you?

MARZELLINE
Why then, we are a pair.

JAQUINO
And in a few weeks we might–

MARZELLINE
This is charming—you are settling the
time. *(Knocking at the door.)*

JAQUINO
The deuce! This eternal knocking!
I was so pleased, but I am always losing the
catch.

MARZELLINE
How tiresome is his love. My hours now
last forever. I know this wretched one is his
own torment; I pity him. But Fidelio is my
choice, and to love him my greatest
delight!

es tut mir so leid auch um ihn! Fidelio hab'
ich gewählet, ihn lieben ist süßer Gewinn.

JAQUINO *(zurückkommend)*
Wo war ich? – sie sieht mich nicht an!

MARZELLINE
Da ist er, – er fängt wieder an!

JAQUINO
Wann wirst du das Jawort mir geben? Es
könnte ja heute noch sein.

MARZELLINE *(bei Seite)*
O weh, er verbittert mein Leben! (zu ihm)
Jetzt, morgen und immer: nein, nein!

JAQUINO
Du bist doch wahrhaftig von Stein; kein
Wünschen, kein Bitten geht ein.

MARZELLINE *(für sich)*
Ich muß ja so hart mit ihm sein.(zu ihm)
Jetzt, morgen und immer: nein, nein! (für
sich) Ich muß ja so hart mit ihm sein, er
hofft bei dem mindesten Schein.

JAQUINO
So wirst du dich nimmer bekehren?
Was meinst du?

MARZELLINE
Du könntest nun gehn!

JAQUINO
Where was I? She does not look at me.

MARZELLINE
There, he starts again.

JAQUINO
When shall you give your consent, and
why not today? You are as hard as a stone.

MARZELLINE
Alas, he embitters my life, now tomorrow,
and always no! I must be firm with him.

JAQUINO
All desires, all entreaties are in vain.

MARZELLINE
I must be firm with him; even a shadow
gives him hope.

JAQUINO
Will you always be stubborn? What say
you?

MARZELLINE
You may go, or stay here.

JAQUINO
Wie? dich anzusehn, willst du mir wehren?
Auch das noch?…

MARZELLINE
So bleibe hier stehn!

JAQUINO
… auch das noch? Du hast mir so oft doch
versprochen – …

MARZELLINE
Versprochen? Nein, das geht zu weit!

JAQUINO
… du hast mir u.s.w. *(Man pocht.)*

JAQUINO
Zum Henker, das ewige Pochen, zum
Henker!

MARZELLINE
So bin ich doch endlich befreit! Das ist ein
willkommener Klang, es wurde zu Tode
mir bang.

JAQUINO
Es ward ihr im Ernste schon bang: wer
weiß, ob es mir nicht gelang?

JAQUINO
What? You even forbid me your sight?
What say you?

MARZELLINE
I promised you?!

JAQUINO
What say you?
You have promised me often – …

MARZELLINE
I promised? No, not so quick.

JAQUINO
…you promised.*(A knock at the door.)*

JAQUINO
The deuce! That eternal knocking!

MARZELLINE
Released at last—that is a welcome sound,
I was frightened to death.

JAQUINO
It's true, she was frightened—but who
knows whether or not I succeeded?

SCENE II

Marzelline (allein)

Marzelline (alone)

disc no. 1/track 3

MARZELLINE

Armer Jaquino, ich war ihm sonst recht
gut, da kam Fidelio in unser Haus und seit
der Zeit ist alles in mir und um mich
verändert.

MARZELLINE

Poor Jaquino, I almost pity him. The compassion I feel for him enhances my love for
Fidelio—he must be fond of me too. If I
know my fathers mind, my happiness
might soon be complete.

disc no. 1/track 4

MARZELLINE

O wär' ich schon mit dir vereint,
und dürfte Mann dich nennen!
Ein Mädchen darf ja, was es meint, zur
Hälfte nur bekennen. Doch wenn ich nicht
erröten muß ob einen warmen Herzen-
skuß, wenn nichts uns stört auf Erden –
(Sie seufzt und legt die Hand auf die
Brust.) Die Hoffnung schon erfüllt die
Brust mit unaussprechlich süßer Lust, wie
glücklich will ich werden! In Ruhe stiller
Häuslichkeit erwach' ich jeden Morgen,
wir grüßen uns mit Zärtlichkeit, der Fleiß
verscheucht die Sorgen. Und ist die Arbeit
abgetan, dann schleicht die holde Nacht
heran, dann ruh'n wir von Beschwerden.
Die Hoffnung u.s.w.

MARZELLINE

Oh, how happy I would be, if in wedlock
united with you, and I would call you my
husband. But silence best becomes a maid-
en in love, they say. But I need not blush
at a kind and heartfelt kiss, where nothing
on earth disturbs the hope that fills my
breast.
Oh what delight! What bliss is mine! How
happy I! Each morn fresh joy does bring,
with fond embrace in union blest, each
others heart we tell, all care we bid fly from
our door, the labor over, fair night
approaches, and brings sweet rest to us.
Oh, what delight, etc.

SCENE III

MARZELLINE, ROCCO, JAQUINO (*Jaquino trägt
Gartenwerkzeug hinter Rocco her und ins Haus.*)

MARZELLINE, ROCCO, JAQUINO (*Coming out
of Rocco's house.*)

disc no. 1/track 5

ROCCO
Marzelline? Marzelline?

MARZELLINE
Vater?

ROCCO
Ist Fidelio noch nicht zurück?
Ich erwarte ihn mit Ungeduld!

MARZELLINE
Da kommt er schon!

SCENE IV

Vorige, Leonore (Sie trägt ein dunkles Wamms, ein rotes Gilet, dunkles Beinkleid, kurze Stiefel, einen breiten Gürtel von schwarzem Leder mit einer kupfernen Schnalle; ihre Haare sind in eine Netzhaube gesteckt. Auf dem Rücken trägt sie ein Behältnis mit Lebensmitteln, auf den Armen Ketten, die sie beim Eintreten an dem Stübchen des Pförtners ablegt; an der Seite hängt ihr eine blecherne Büchse an einer Schnur.)

ROCCO
Armer Fidelio! Diesmal hast du dir zuviel aufgeladen. Die Ketten, sind sie jetzt gut gemacht?

LEONORE
Gewiß, recht gut und stark. Keiner der Gefangenen wird sie je zerbrechen.

ROCCO
Wieviel kostet alles zusammen?

ROCCO
Marzelline? Marzelline?

MARZELLINE
Father?

ROCCO
Is Fidelio not back?
I am growing impatient!

MARZELLINE
He's coming soon!

(Same as above. Leonore enters, carrying on her back a large basket with provisions and fetters on her arms, which she places in the gatekeeper's room. A tin box hangs from her waist by a ribbon..)

ROCCO
Poor Fidelio! This time, you have burdened yourself too much. What have you brought?

LEONORE
I must admit, I am a little fatigued

ROCCO
What is the amount, altogether?

LEONORE

Hier ist die genaue Rechnung.

ROCCO

Gut! – Brav! Du kaufst alles wohlfeiler als ich. Sei versichert, dein Lohn soll nicht ausbleiben.

LEONORE

O glaubt nicht, daß ich meine Schuldigkeit nur des Lohnes wegen...

ROCCO

Still! Meinst du, ich könnte dir nicht ins Herz sehen?

LEONORE

Here is the exact account.

ROCCO

Good, well done! You buy things cheaper than I. You are earning my favor—be assured you will be rewarded.

LEONORE

Oh, don't think I fulfill my duties for the sake of a reward…

ROCCO

Hush! Do you think I don't know what's in your heart?

disc no. 1/track 6 *Quartett* With this quartet, Beethoven leaves the Singspiel form entirely for the first time in the opera and enters the Romantic era. "Mir ist. " starts in the lower strings, with a beautiful but clearly sad melody that could be the start of the slow movement of one of the composer's late symphonies. This is a total change from what we've heard previously. Leonore has entered the picture and the true seriousness of the opera's situation takes over. There is a wonderful still-ness to it, with all four characters singing softly. Each has his or her own feelings to express, and it's interesting to note that Leonore's vocal line, which will show itself to be far more complicated and sophisticated later, mimics Marzelline's and the others': She's hiding her true identity and when she interacts with these people she fits right in, vocally. She conceals her own noble birth and her "differ-entness."

MARZELLINE (*welche während des Lobes, das Rocco Leonore erteilte, die größte Teilnahme hat blicken lassen und sie mit immer zunehmender Bewegung liebevoll betrachtet hat; für sich*)
Mir ist so wunderbar, es engt das Herz mir ein; er liebt mich, es ist klar, ich werde glücklich sein!

MARZELLINE (*while Rocco is commending Leonore, Marzelline is focused on her, and gazes on her with continually increasing emotion.*)
This is so wonderful, my heart is oppressed. He loves me, it's clear I shall be happy.

LEONORE *(für sich)*
Wie groß ist die Gefahr, wie schwach der
Hoffnung Schein! Sie liebt mich, es ist klar,
o namenlose Pein!

ROCCO *(der während dessen wieder auf die
Vorderbühne zurückgekehrt ist; für sich)*
Sie liebt ihn, es ist klar, ja, Mädchen, er
wird dein! Ein gutes junges Paar, sie werden glücklich sein!

JAQUINO *(der unter dem Beobachten sich immer
mehr genähert hat, auf der Seite und etwas hinter
den Übrigen stehend; für sich)*
Mir sträubt sich schon das Haar, der Vater
willigt ein, mir wird so wunderbar, mir fällt
kein Mittel ein! (Nach Endigung dieses
Kanons geht Jaquino in seine Stube
zurück.)

LEONORE
Oh, what danger. Hope is in vain—she
loves me, what pain.

ROCCO
She loves him, it's clear; yes, girl he is
yours. A good young couple; they shall be
happy.

JAQUINO
My hair stands on end—her father consents; I don't know how I am nor what to
do.

disc no. 1/track 7

ROCCO
Höre Fidelio! Wenn ich auch nicht weiß,
wie und wo du auf die Welt gekommen
bist, und wenn du auch gar keinen Vater
gehabt hättest, ich weiß doch was ich tue.
Ich mache dich zu meinem Tochtermann.

MARZELLINE
Vater, wirst du es bald tun?

ROCCO
Sobald der Gouverneur nach Sevilla gereist
sein wird, gebe ich euch zusammen. Nun,
ihr habt euch doch recht herzlich lieb,

ROCCO
Hark, Fidelio! Though I don't know how
and where you were born, and if you
haven't had any father at all, yet I know
what I think: I make you my son-in-law.

MARZELLINE
Father, is this true?

ROCCO
As soon as the governor has set out for
Seville, we have more leisure; you know he
goes there every month to give account of

69

nicht wahr? Aber das ist doch nicht alles, was zu einer guten Haushaltung gehört. Man braucht auch... (Er macht die Geberde des Geldzählens.)

all that occurs in the prison. In a few days, he must be off again. The day after his departure, I give you to each other—you may depend on that.

disc no. 1/track 9 The rhythm and tune of Rocco's aria are jaunty and rustic; this could be a drinking song. Rocco is the only character who changes in the course of the opera—later, in the dungeon scene in Act II, when his situation is dreadful, we find none of this unrefined music.

ROCCO
Hat man nicht auch Gold beineben, kann man nicht ganz glücklich sein; traurig schleppt sich fort das Leben, mancher Kummer stellt sich ein. Doch wenn's in der Taschen fein klingelt und rollt, da hält man das Schicksal gefangen; und Macht und Liebe verschafft dir das Gold und stillet das kühnste Verlangen. Das Glück dient wie ein Knecht für Sold, es ist ein schönes Ding, das Gold. Wenn sich Nichts mit Nichts verbindet, ist und bleibt die Summe klein; wer bei Tisch nur Liebe findet, wird nach Tische hungrig sein. Drum lächle der Zufall euch gnädig und hold, und segne und lenk' euer Streben, das Liebchen im Arme, im Beutel das Gold, so mögt ihr viel Jahre durchleben. Das Glück dient u.s.w.

ROCCO
If we have no money, love cannot bring comfort. Sadly, life drags on, and sorrow follows. But when the coin jingles in the pockets, then fate is our prisoner. Yes, gold brings love and power, and fills our wishes. Happiness is the slave of gold; oh what a precious thing is gold! Nothing with nothing united, what remains? At dinner sweet love, and after dinner hunger; may fate smile upon you and bless your endeavors. Arm in arm, plenty of money in the purse; many a year may you thus live. Yes, happiness is subservient to gold; oh what a precious thing is gold1

LEONORE
Ihr habt recht, Vater Rocco, aber es gibt noch etwas, das mir nicht weniger kostbar wäre.

LEONORE
It is easy to say, Father Rocco, but there is something that would be just as valuable to me.

ROCCO
Und das wäre?

ROCCO
What is this?

LEONORE

Euer Vertrauen. Wie oft sehe ich Euch ganz ermattet aus den unterirdischen Gewölben zurückkehren. Warum erlaubt Ihr mir nicht Euch dorthin zu begleiten?

ROCCO

Du weißt, daß ich den strengsten Befehl habe, niemanden – wer es auch sein mag – zu den Staatsgefangenen zu lassen. Niemanden!

MARZELLINE

Du arbeitest dich ja zu Tode, lieber Vater.

ROCCO

Ja, ja, ihr habt recht. Diese schwere Arbeit würde mir doch endlich zuviel werden. Der Gouverneur muß mir erlauben, dich in die geheimen Kerker mit mir zu nehmen. Indes gibt es ein Gewölbe, in das ich dich nie führen werde.

MARZELLINE

Wo der Gefangene sitzt, von dem du schon oft gesprochen hast?

ROCCO

Ja, ja.

LEONORE

Ist es schon lange her, daß er gefangen ist?

ROCCO

Schon über zwei Jahre.

LEONORE

Your confidence. Pardon the reproach, but I see you return from the underground vaults, out of breath and spent with fatigue. Why don't you allow me to accompany you there?

ROCCO

You know, however, that I have the strictest orders not to admit anyone to the state prisoners.

MARZELLINE

But there are are too many prisoners here—you work yourself to death, father.

ROCCO

Yes, you are right. The heavy labor would, in the end, be too much for me. The governor is very strict, but he must permit me to take you into the secret dungeons.

MARZELLINE

Down to where the prisoner is, of whom you have spoken?

ROCCO

Yes, yes.

LEONORE

It has been a long time since he has been in prison?

ROCCO

It has been over two years.

LEONORE
Zwei Jahre! Er muß ein großer Verbrecher sein.

ROCCO
Oder er muß große Feinde haben, das kommt ungefähr auf eins heraus. Nun, es kann nicht mehr lange mit ihm dauern. Seit einem Monat muß ich auf Befehl Pizarros seine Portionen kleiner machen. Jetzt hat er binnen vierundzwanzig Stunden nicht mehr als zwei Unzen schwarzes Brot und eine halbe Maß Wasser. Kein Licht – kein Stroh – nichts.

LEONORE
Großer Gott!

MARZELLINE
Vater, führe Fidelio ja nicht zu ihm. Diesen Anblick könnte er nicht ertragen.

LEONORE
Warum denn nicht? Ich habe Mut und Kraft!

ROCCO
Gut, Söhnchen, gut, hab' immer Mut, dann wird's dir auch gelingen; das Herz wird hart durch Gegenwart bei fürchterlichen Dingen.

LEONORE
Two years! He must be a great criminal.

ROCCO
Or he must have great enemies—that means nearly the same thing. But, it is best for people like us to know as few secrets as possible, therefore I have never listened to him. I might have gossiped to my injury without doing him any good. But, he will not much longer plague me—he cannot last much longer.

LEONORE
Good God!

MARZELLINE
Father, do not take Fidelio to him, he could not bear the sight.

LEONORE
Why not? I have courage and nerve enough!

ROCCO
Good, my son, good. Be ever of good cheer, then you will succeed. The heart gets hardened when in often contact with horrible scenes.

BEETHOVEN AT AGE 47, IN A DRAWING BY A. VON KLOEBER

LEONORE

Ich habe Mut! Mit kaltem Blut will ich hinab mich wagen. Für hohen Lohn kann Liebe schon auch hohe Leiden tragen.

MARZELLINE

Dein gutes Herz wird manchen Schmerz in diesen Grüften leiden; dann kehrt zurück der Liebe Glück und unnennbare Freuden.

ROCCO

Du wirst dein Glück ganz sicher bauen.

LEONORE

Ich hab' auf Gott und Recht Vertrauen.

MARZELLINE

Du darfst mir auch in's Auge schauen; der Liebe Macht ist auch nicht klein, ja, wir werden glücklich sein!

LEONORE

Ja, ich kann noch glücklich sein!

ROCCO

Ja, ihr werdet glücklich sein! Der Gouverneur soll heut' erlauben, daß du mit mir die Arbeit teilst.

LEONORE

Du wirst mir alle Ruhe rauben, wenn du bis morgen nur verweilst.

LEONORE

I have courage, with calmness will I venture down, for high reward. Love will endure high suffering, too.

MARZELLINE

Your good heart will suffer woefully in those dread vaults, but the joys of love await you in return, and happiness will be yours.

ROCCO

Your fortune is in your own hands, young man.

LEONORE

I confide in God and all that is right.

MARZELLINE

You may see in my eyes, that love's power is not small.

LEONORE

Yes, we shall all be happy.

ROCCO

Yes, we shall be happy. The governor consents today that you shall share my duty.

LEONORE

You destroy my rest if you delay until tomorrow.

MARZELLINE
Ja, guter Vater, bitt' ihn heute, in Kurzem sind wir dann ein Paar.

ROCCO
Ja, der Gouverneur u.s.w. Ich bin ja bald des Grabes Beute; ich brauche Hilf', es ist ja wahr!

LEONORE *(für sich)*
Wie lang' bin ich des Kummers Beute! Du, Hoffnung, reichst mir Labung dar!

MARZELLINE
(zärtlich gegen ihren Vater)
Ach, lieber Vater! was fällt euch ein? Lang Freund und Rater müßt ihr uns sein!

ROCCO
Nur auf der Hut, dann geht es gut, gestillt wird euer Sehnen! Gebt euch die Hand und schließt das Band in süßen Freudentränen!

MARZELLINE
O habe Mut! O welche Glut, o welch ein tiefes Sehnen! Ein festes Band mit Herz und Hand! O süße, süße Tränen!

LEONORE
Ihr seid so gut, ihr macht mir Mut, gestillt wird bald mein Sehnen! (für sich) Ich gab die Hand zum süßen Band, es kostet bitt're Tränen!

MARZELLINE
Yes, good Father, take him today, the sooner is our union.

ROCCO
Yes the governor consents, I shall soon go down to my grave and it's true that I need help.

LEONORE
A long time have I been prey to woe, a ray of hope now fills me.

MARZELLINE
Ah, good Father, what do you think? Long, long, you'll be our friend and comfort.

ROCCO
Be prudent and if all goes well, your wishes will be granted.
Shake hands and be united, in sweet tears of joy.

MARZELLINE
Oh have courage, oh what order, what deep feeling. A lasting tie with hand and heart, oh sweet and welcome tears.

LEONORE
You are so good, you inspire me with courage, my desire is fulfilled.
I have given my sacred pledge—ah what bitter tears it costs me.

Scene V

Rocco, Pizarro, Offiziere, Wachen

Rocco, Pizarro, Officers, Guards

(Während des zuvor begonnenen Marsches wird das Haupttor durch Schildwachen von außen geöffnet. Offiziere ziehen mit einem Detachement ein, dann kommt Pizarro, das Tor wird wieder geschlossen. – Unter Musik.)

(During the March, the principal gate opens from without; Officers with a detachment enter, then Pizarro. The gate is closed.)

Pizarro *(zu den Offizieren)*
Drei Schildwachen auf den Wall, sechs Mann auf den Turm. Jeder, der sich der Festung nähert, werde so- gleich zu mir gebracht! – Ist etwas Neues vorgefallen?

Pizarro *(to the Officers)*
Three guards on the rampart, six day and night on the drawbridge, the same number on the side of the garden. Whoever comes near, bring them to me. *(to Rocco)*
Rocco, has anything new happened.

Rocco
Nein, Herr!

Rocco
No, Sir.

Pizarro
Die Depeschen!

Pizarro
Where are the dispatches?

Rocco
Hier.

Rocco
Here.

Pizarro
Empfehlungen, Vorwürfe... Diese Schrift kenne ich. "Der Minister hat in Erfahrung gebracht, daß die Staatsgefängnisse mehrere Opfer willkürlicher Gewalt entalten. Er reist morgen ab, um Sie mit einer Unter suchung zu Überraschen." – Wenn er entdeckte, daß ich diesen Florestan in Ketten liegen habe, ihn, den er längst tot glaubt... doch es gibt ein Mittel.

Pizarro
Commands, reprimands. What do we have here? "The minister has learned that among the prisoners under your charge, several are victims of arbitrary power; he departs tomorrow to surprise you with an examination. Be on your guard, and try to keep things together."– Ah! If he discovers that I have Florestan lying here in chains, whom he has long ago thought dead! One bold deed can and must alleviate my anxieties.

The strings begin absolutely frantically with Pizarro's musical entrance, jagged, abnormal, angular utterances unlike anything we've heard before. He practically spits his words out, and each note is an exclamation. This vile little tyrant upsets goodness with his music as he does with his words and deeds. The rhythms in his aria keep changing—he may represent the police, but his policing is corrupt and does not bring either order or peace.

PIZARRO

Ha! welch ein Augenblick! Die Rache werd' ich kühlen! Dich rufet dein Geschick! In seinem Herzen wühlen, o Wonne, großes Glück! Schon war ich nah', im Staube, dem lauten Spott zum Raube, dahingestreckt zu sein. Nun ist es mir geworden, den Mörder selbst zu morden! Ha! welch' ein Augenblick u.s.w. Nun ist er mir u.s.w. in seiner letzen Stunde, den Stahl in seiner Wunde, ihm noch ins Ohr zu schrein: Triumph! der Sieg ist mein!

DIE WACHE *(halblaut unter sich)*
Er spricht von Tod und Wunde, nun fort auf unsre Runde! Wie wichtig muß es sein! Er spricht von Tod und Wunde! – Wacht scharf auf eurer Runde!

PIZARRO

Ah, what a moment1 Yes, I'll be revenged. Your fate calls! Yes, I'll pierce his hears. Oh, Joy! High delight! Already I was crouched in dust, a prey to base mockery stretched on the ground. But, now it is mine to kill him that would have killed me. In his last hour, the steel in his bosom. Yes, I cry aloud in his ear: triumph! Victory is mine!

THE GUARDS *(among themselves)*
He speaks of death and vengeance. Watch carefully, and mind well on your rounds— it must be important.

PIZARRO

Hauptmann! Besteigen Sie mit einem Trompeter so- gleich den Turm der Festung. Achten Sie mit größter Aufmerksamkeit auf die Straße von Sevilla. Sobald Sie einen Wagen sehen, lassen Sie augenblicklich ein Signal geben, hören Sie? Augenblicklich! Sie haften mir mit ihrem Kopf dafür. – Auf eure Posten!! – Rocco!

PIZARRO

Captain! Ascend the tower with a trumpeter. Look with great attention toward the high road to Seville. As soon as you see a carriage surrounded by riders, signal me immediately. You answer for this with your head. Guards: away to your posts! Rocco!

ROCCO
Herr?!

ROCCO
Sir?!

disc no. 1/track 15

PIZARRO
Jetzt, Alter, jetzt hat es Eile! Dir wird ein
Glück zu Teile, du wirst ein reicher Mann,
(Wirft ihm einen Beutel zu.) das geb' ich
nur daran.

ROCCO
So sagt doch nur in Eile, womit ich dienen
kann.

PIZARRO
Du bist von kaltem Blute, von unverza-
gtem Mute durch langen Dienst geworden.

ROCCO
Was soll ich? Redet, redet!

PIZARRO
Morden!

ROCCO (ERSCHRECKT)
Wie?

PIZARRO
Höre mich nur an! Du bebst? bist du ein
Mann? – Wir dürfen gar nicht säumen,
dem Staate liegt daran, den bösen Untertan
schnell aus dem Weg zu räumen.

ROCCO
O Herr! …

PIZARRO
Now, old friend, your fortune's made.
You are a man of riches.
(Gives him a purse.)
This is only to start.

ROCCO
Oh, quick, tell me what I can do for you?

PIZARRO
You are of old blood, of undaunted courage
from long service.

ROCCO
Tell me! What can I do?

PIZARRO
Kill.

ROCCO (ALARMED)
Who?

PIZARRO
Listen, you tremble! Are you a man? We
must delay no longer. On account of the
state, a subject so bad must be gotten rid of.

ROCCO
Oh, sir! …

PIZARRO

Du stehst noch an? … (für sich) Er darf nicht länger leben, sonst ist's um mich gescheh'n. Pizarro sollte beben? Du fällst, ich werde steh'n.

ROCCO

Die Glieder fühl' ich beben, wie könnt' ich das besteh'n? Ich nehm' ihm nicht das Leben, mag, was da will, gescheh'n. Nein, Herr, das Leben nehmen, das ist nicht meine Pflicht.

PIZARRO

Ich will mich selbst bequemen, wenn dir's an Mut gebricht. Nun eile rasch und munter zu jenem Mann hinunter, du weißt, du weißt –

ROCCO

Der kaum mehr lebt, und wie ein Schatten schwebt?

PIZARRO (*mit Grimm*)

Zu dem, zu dem hinab! Ich wart' in kleiner Ferne, du gräbst in der Cisterne sehr schnell ein Grab.

ROCCO

Und dann? und dann?

PIZARRO

Dann werd' ich selbst vermummt mich in den Kerker schleichen: (Er zeigt den Dolch.) ein Stoß – und er verstummt!

PIZARRO

You still hesitate? …
(aside) He must live no longer, or I'm undone. Ha! Pizarro should live in far? No! You die, I stand.

ROCCO

I am trembling. How could I bear it? No, I'll not take his life, let happen what may. Sir, I am not bound in duty to kill.

PIZARRO

I'll do it myself if your courage fails. Only quick. Hasten down to the man.

ROCCO

Who scarcely lives the semblance of a shadow.

PIZARRO

Yes, to him, to him in the dungeon. I'll wait at a distance. And quickly, prepare him a grave in the cistern.

ROCCO

And then?

PIZARRO

You give a signal, and I'll descend into the dungeon. (He draws a dagger.) One blow—and he is finished!

Rocco

Verhungernd in den Ketten, ertrug er lange Pein. Ihn töten heißt ihn retten, der Dolch wird ihn befrei'n.

Pizarro

Er sterb' in seinen Ketten, zu kurz war seine Pein! Sein Tod nur kann mich retten, dann werd' ich ruhig sein. Jetzt, Alter, jetzt hat es Eile! Hast du mich verstanden? Du giebst ein Zeichen; dann werd' ich selbst vermummt mich in den Kerker schleichen: ein Stoß – und er verstummt!

Rocco

Verhungernd in den Ketten u.s.w.

Pizarro

Er sterb' in seinen Ketten u.s.w. (Pizarro ab gegen den Garten, Rocco folgt ihm.)

Rocco

Starving in chains, his suffering is great, to kill him is to save him, and mine the rest.

Pizarro

Starving in chains, his suffering is great, to kill him is to save him, and mine the rest. You give a signal, and I'll descend into the dungeon.
One blow—and he is finished!
 Etc.

Rocco

Starving in chains, etc.

Pizarro

Starving in chains, etc
(Pizarro exits toward the garden, Rocco follows.)

Scene VI

Leonore *(allein)*
(Sie tritt in heftiger innerer Bewegung von der andern Seite auf und sieht den Abgehenden mit steigender Unruhe nach.)

Leonore *(alone)*
(She appears, agitated, from the opposite side; she watches everyone leaving with increasing anxiety.)

disc no. 1/track 16   Leonore's big scene comes right on the heels of the previous duet; Beethoven wanted no pause whatsoever as Leonore can barely contain herself. The aria is introduced by low stabbing strings as she expresses hatred for the villain, but soon gives way to a prayer-like expression, with horn accompaniment, where she hopes for internal calm. It then launches into a faster section filled with resolve: Her voice runs strongly from top to bottom and finally reaches a triumphant high B on the all-important word "married love." This aria introduces a voice type that requires great agility as well as great power to exclaim throughout its large range; it is here that we realize, almost through Leonore's vocal line alone, how noble and strong she is. This great, powerful lyricism is almost spiritual and is later to be noted in Florestan's aria as well—they are one-and-the-same—aristocratic. Since she is not being heard by any of the other characters she's free to take wing, vocally and emotionally; we see now that she is indeed heroic.

LEONORE

Abscheulicher! wo eilst du hin? Was hast du vor – in wildem Grimme? Des Mitleids Ruf, – der Menschheit Stimme, – (heftig) rührt nichts mehr deinen Tigersinn? Doch toben auch wie Meereswogen dir in der Seele Zorn und Wut, so leuchtet mir ein Farbenbogen, der hell auf dunkeln Wolken ruht. Der blickt so still, so friedlich nieder, der spiegelt alte Zeiten wieder, und neu besänftigt wallt mein Blut. Komm, Hoffnung, laß den letzten Stern der Müden nicht erbleichen! O komm, erhell' mein Ziel, sei's noch so fern, die Liebe, sie wird's erreichen. Komm, o komm u.s.w. Ich folg' dem innern Triebe, ich wanke nicht, mich stärkt die Pflicht der treuen Gattenliebe. O du, für den ich alles trug, könnt' ich zur Stelle dringen, wo Bosheit dich in Fesseln schlug, und süßen Trost dir bringen! Ich folg' dem innern Triebe u.s.w.

(Ab gegen den Garten.)

LEONORE

Monster! Where are you going in such a hurry? What scheme breeds your rage? Nor pity's call, nor humanity's voice, nothing moves your tiger mind. Yet, I see the storm of passion rages within your soul, but I still see a ray of hope on heaven's face; It brings me calm, restores my soul; In fond recollection of past happiness my heart now beats anew.

Sweet hope, forsake not this lingering heart! Oh, let a ray of joy console my sorrowing love. See, my bosom beats, I hesitate not—yes, a wife devout—I bring—fresh vigor.

(Exit into the garden.)

SCENE VII

MARZELLINE, JAQUINO
(Marzelline kommt aus dem Hause, Jaquino ihr nach.)

MARZELLINE, JAQUINO
(Marzelline, from the house, Jaquino follows her.)

JAQUINO
Marzelline! Marzelline!!

MARZELLINE
Nein! Nein, ich will nicht!

SCENE VIII

Die Vorigen, Rocco, Leonore (aus dem Garten)

ROCCO
Was habt ihr beide denn nun wieder zu
zanken?

MARZELLINE
Ach, er will, daß ich ihn heiraten soll.

JAQUINO
Ja, sie soll mich lieben, sie soll mich wenig-
stens heiraten!

ROCCO
Nein Jaquino! Von einer Heirat kann jetzt
keine Rede sein. Mich beschäftigen andere,
wichtigere Dinge.

LEONORE
Vater Rocco, Ihr verspracht mir so oft, einmal die Gefangenen in den Festungsgarten
zu lassen. Heute ist das Wetter so schön!

JAQUINO
Marzelline! Marzelline!!

MARZELLINE
No! Not a word!

The former, Rocco, Leonore (from the garden)

ROCCO
Are you quarreling again?

MARZELLINE
Ah—he constantly teases me, he wants me
to marry him.

JAQUINO
Yes, she is my darling—we will marry!

ROCCO
No, Jaquino. I have raised my only daughter with care for a gentlemen. No, my
mind is full of other thoughts.

LEONORE
Father Rocco, I've begged you to allow the
poor prisoners to walk in the fresh air.
Today the weather is fine; the governor
does not come yet.

ROCCO
Kinder! – Ohne Erlaubnis des Gou-
verneurs?

MARZELLINE
Aber er sprach doch so lange mit dir. Vielleicht solltest du ihm einen Gefallen tun?

ROCCO
Einen Gefallen? Du hast recht. – Auf diese
Gefahr hin kann ich es wagen. – Jaquino!
Fidelio! Öffnet die leichteren Gefängnisse.
Ich aber gehe zu Pizarro und halte ihn
zurück, indem ich für dein Bestes rede.
(Rocco ab. – Leonore und Jaquino
schließen die wohlverwahrten Gefäng-
nißtüren auf, ziehen sich dann mit
Marzelline in den Hintergrund und
beobachten mit Teilnahme die nach und
nach auftretenden Gefangenen.)

ROCCO
Children, without the permission of the
governor?

MARZELLINE
But perhaps you are to do him a favor—
then he will not be so particular.

ROCCO
A favor? You are right, Marzelline. On this
risk, I may venture it. Well then, Jaquino
and Fidelio, go and open the minor cells
and I will go to Pizarro and delay him.
(Rocco leaves. Leonore and Jaquino open
the gates of the prison, the retire with
Marzelline in the background and observe
the prisoners with sympathy.)

SCENE IX

Die Vorigen, Erster und Zweiter Gefangenen, die
Gefangenen (Während des Ritornells kommen die
Gefangenen nach und nach auf die Bühne.)

The above, Chorus of Prisoners

disc no. 1/track 18   The prisoners are let out of their cells to the strains of generous, long musical
phrases. Two prisoners offer individual utterances, but they speak for all and
they all go gently into the garden. Rocco and Leonore have a quick but important (to the plot) conversational duet in which Leonore is first told that Pizarro
has given permission for her to marry Marzelline, and then, more crucially, that
today will be the day she's allowed into the dungeon, and therefore will see her
husband. But excitement turns to horror when she realizes that it's to kill him—
she (and her music) turn frantic and fearful—and even Rocco realizes how
deeply doing such a deed affects Leonore. With the return of Pizarro the tempo

picks up manically with his jagged rhythms, and the prisoners are made to return to their cells. In a marchlike, definitive rhythm, they do so as the act ends very quietly, but hardly peacefully, to the ominous sound of softly played kettle-drums. The act, which began in light, has ended in darkness.

DIE GEFANGENEN
O welche Lust, in freier Luft den Atem
leicht zu heben! O welche Lust! Nur hier,
nur hier ist Leben, der Kerker eine Gruft!
O welche Lust u.s.w.

ERSTER GEFANGENER
Wir wollen mit Vertrauen
auf Gottes Hilfe bauen,
die Hoffnung flüstert sanft mir zu:
Wir werden frei, wir finden Ruh'.

DIE GEFANGENEN *(jeder für sich)*
O Himmel! Rettung! welch' ein Glück!
O Freiheit, kehrst du zurück?
(Hier erscheint ein Offizier auf dem Walle
und entfernt sich wieder.)

ZWEITER GEFANGENER
Sprecht leise, haltet euch zurück!
Wir sind belauscht mit Ohr und Blick!
(Ehe der Chor noch ganz geendet ist,
erscheint Rocco im Hintergrunde der
Bühne, und redet angelegentlich mit
Leonore. Die Gefangenen entfernen sich in
den Garten; Rocco und Leonore
nähern sich der Vorderbühne.)

PRISONERS
Oh what pleasure, to breathe the fresh air
of heaven! Here only is to live, the dungeon is a tomb.

A PRISONER
Let us trust in heaven with confidence!
Hope softly whispers: "You will be free,
you will have peace."

PRISONERS *(among themselves)*
Oh heaven! Deliverance! What a blessing!
Oh Liberty returns?

ANOTHER PRISONER
Speak softly—restrain yourselves. We are
watched by eyes and ears.

SCENE X

Rocco, Leonore

Rocco, Leonore

LEONORE
Nun sprecht, wie ging's?

ROCCO
Recht gut, recht gut!
Zusammen rafft' ich meinen Mut
und trug ihm alles vor;
und sollt'st du's glauben,
was er zur Antwort mir gab? –
Die Heirat, und daß du mir hilfst, will er
erlauben;
noch heute führ' ich in den Kerker dich
hinab.

LEONORE *(ausbrechend)*
Noch heute, noch heute? –
O welch' ein Glück, o welche Wonne!

ROCCO
Ich sehe deine Freude!
Nur noch ein Augenblick,
dann gehen wir schon Beide –

LEONORE
Wohin, wohin?

ROCCO
– zu jenem Mann hinab,
dem ich seit vielen Wochen
stets weniger zu essen gab.

LEONORE
Ha! wird er losgesprochen?

ROCCO
O nein!

LEONORE
Now speak, how did you succeed?

ROCCO
Very well, very well. I composed my mind
and mentioned everything. And would you
believe it? That he gave the answer? He
allows the marriage and that you assist me.
This very day you shall go with me to the
dungeons.

LEONORE *(breaking forth)*
Today! What happiness!

ROCCO
I can see your joy. Only another moment
and we both will go.

LEONORE
Where?

ROCCO
Down to that man whom for weeks past I
have continually starved.

LEONORE
Ah! Is he also freed?

ROCCO
Oh no!

85

LEONORE
So sprich, so sprich!

ROCCO
O nein, o nein!
(geheimnißvoll) Wir müssen ihn, doch
wie? – befrei'n!
Er muß in einer Stunde –
den Finger auf dem Munde –
von uns begraben sein.

LEONORE
So ist er tot?

ROCCO
Noch nicht, noch nicht!

LEONORE (*zurückfahrend*)
Ist ihn zu töten deine Pflich?

ROCCO
Nein, guter Junge, zitt're nicht,
zum Morden dingt sich Rocco nicht, nein –!
Der Gouverneur kommt selbst hinab,
wir beide graben nur das Grab.

LEONORE (*bei Seite*)
Vielleicht das Grab des Gatten graben?
Was kann fürchterlicher sein! Was!

ROCCO
Ich darf ihn nicht mit Speise laben,
ihm wird im Grabe besser sein.
Wir müssen gleich zu Werke schreiten,
du mußt mir helfen, mich begleiten,
hart ist des Kerkermeisters Brot.

LEONORE
He's free, he's free?

ROCCO
Oh no, oh no!
(mysteriously) We—well, yes, we must free
him!
Your lips are closed—he must be in his
grave.

LEONORE
So he is dead?

ROCCO
Not yet, not yet!

LEONORE (*starting back*)
And must you kill him?

ROCCO
No, my fine fellow, never fear. Rocco is no
murderer. The governor himself comes
down—we only dig the grave.

LEONORE (*aside*)
What could be more horrible? To dig the
grave of a husband..oh!

ROCCO
I dare not nourish him; in the grave he
finds rest. We must proceed to work. You
must help and accompany me. The goaler's
bread is hard.

LEONORE
Ich folge dir, wär's in den Tod.

ROCCO
In der zerfallenen Zisterne
bereiten wir die Grube leicht;
ich tu' es, glaube mir, nicht gerne;
auch dir ist schaurig, wie mich deucht?

LEONORE
Ich bin es nur noch nicht gewohnt.

ROCCO
Ich hätte gerne dich verschont,
doch wird es mir allein zu schwer,
und gar so streng ist unser Herr.

LEONORE *(für sich)*
O welch' ein Schmerz!

ROCCO *(für sich)*
Mir scheint, er weine.
(laut) Nein, du bleibst hier, – ich geh'
alleine.

LEONORE *(innig sich an ihn klammernd)*
O nein, o nein!
Ich muß ihn sehn, den Armen sehen,
und müßt ich selbst zu Grunde gehen!

ROCCO
Nein, du bleibst hier!

LEONORE UND ROCCO
So säumen wir nun länger nicht,
wir folgen unsrer strengen Pflicht.

LEONORE
I follow you, till death.

ROCCO
In the old cistern, we'll dig the grave with
ease, believe me I don't like it and you seem
to shudder too.

LEONORE
I'm quite prepared, confide in me.

ROCCO
I willingly would have spared you this, but,
alone, the work's too much.

LEONORE *(to herself)*
Oh what grief!

ROCCO *(aside)*
I think he weeps. (aloud) No, you stay
here. I go alone.

LEONORE *(clinging to him)*
Oh no, oh no!
I must see him, the wretched man, even on
my own peril.

ROCCO
No, remain here!

LEONORE AND ROCCO
Then let's delay no longer, we follow duty's
call.

SCENE XI

Vorige, Jaquino und Marzelline

MARZELLINE
Ach, Vater, Vater, eilt!

ROCCO
Was hast du denn?

JAQUINO
Nicht länger weilt!

ROCCO
Was ist geschehn?

MARZELLINE
Voll Zorn folgt mir Pizarro nach, er drohet
dir.

JAQUINO
Nicht länger weilt!

ROCCO
Gemach, gemach!

LEONORE
So eilet fort!

ROCCO
Nur noch dies Wort: sprich, weiß er schon?

JAQUINO
Ja, er weiß es schon.

The former, Jaquino and Marzelline

MARZELLINE
Oh, father, hurry!

ROCCO
What's the matter?

JAQUINO
Wait no longer!

ROCCO
What has happened?

MARZELLINE
Filled with rage, Pizarro follows me and
threatens you at every step.

JAQUINO
Wait no longer!

ROCCO
Quiet, quiet!

LEONORE
Let's hurry!

ROCCO
Just one word—he knows, then?

JAQUINO
Yes, he knows..

MARZELLINE
Der Offizier sagt' ihm, was wir
jetzt den Gefangenen gewähren.

MARZELLINE
The officer told him of the new indulgence
the prisoners have.

ROCCO
Laßt alle schnell zurücke kehren!

ROCCO
They all must quickly return.

(Jaquino ab in den Garten.)

Jaquino exits.

MARZELLINE
Ihr wißt ja, wie er tobet, und kennet seine
Wut.

MARZELLINE
You know how he rages, and know his fury.

LEONORE
Wie mir's im Innern tobet, empöret ist
mein Blut!

LEONORE
How my heart beats—my soul is at arms!

ROCCO
Mein Herz hat mich gelobet,
sei der Tyrann in Wut!
(Marzelline eilt Jaquino nach.)

ROCCO
My heart rejoices, let the tyrant rave.

SCENE XII

Rocco, Leonore, Pizarro, Zweiter Offizier, Wachen

Rocco, Leonore, Pizarro, an Officer

PIZARRO
Verweg'ner Alter, welche Rechte
legst du dir frevelnd selber bei?
Und ziemt es dem gedung'nen Knechte,
zu geben die Gefang'nen frei?

PIZARRO
Audacious old man! What rights are you
assuming? Does it become the hireling ser-
vant to deliver the prisoners?

ROCCO *(verlegen)*
O Herr!

ROCCO *(embarrassed)*
O Sir!

PIZARRO
Wohlan, wohlan!

ROCCO (eine Entschuldigung suchend)
Des Frühlings Kommen,
das heit're warme Sonnenlicht, dann –
(sich fassend) habt ihr wohl in Acht
genommen,
was sonst zu meinem Vorteil spricht?
(die Mütze abnehmend)
Des Königs Namensfest ist heute,
das feiern wir auf solche Art.
(geheim zu Pizarro)
Der unten stirbt, – doch laßt die Andern
jetzt fröhlich hin und wieder wandern;
für Jenen sei der Zorn gespart!

PIZARRO (leise)
So eile, ihm sein Grab zu graben,
hier will ich stille Ruhe haben.
Schließ' die Gefang'nen wieder ein, –
mögst du nie mehr verwegen sein!

SCENE XIII

Die Vorigen, Marzelline, Jaquino,
die Gefangenen (aus dem Garten)

DIE GEFANGENEN
Leb' wohl, du warmes Sonnenlicht,
schnell schwindest du uns wieder!
Schon sinkt die Nacht hernieder,
aus der so bald kein Morgen bricht!

PIZARRO
Well, well…

ROCCO (Seeking an excuse)
The coming of spring, the serene ray of the
sun, besides, consider what pleads in my
favor. (recovering himself)
Our gracious king's birthday—we celebrate.(secretly to Pizarro)
The one below dies, but suffer the others a
happy hour in the free air; reserve your
fury for him alone!

PIZARRO (softly)
Then hasten to dig his grave; here all must
be quiet. Shut up again the prisoners and
never be so daring again!

The above, Marzelline, Jaquino,
The Prisoners (from the garden)

THE PRISONERS
Farewell warm ray of the sun, soon you'll
vanish again. Night breaks upon us, and
never to behold again the morn.

MARZELLINE *(die Gefangenen betrachtend)*
Wie eilten sie zum Sonnenlicht, und scheiden traurig wieder! (für sich) Die Andern murmeln nieder, hier wohnt die Lust, die Freude nicht!

LEONORE *(zu den Gefangenen)*
Ihr hört das Wort, drum zögert nicht, kehrt in den Kerker wieder! (für sich) Angst rinnt durch meine Glieder; ereilt den Frevler kein Gericht?

JAQUINO *(zu den Gefangenen)*
Ihr hört das Wort, drum zögert nicht, kehrt in den Kerker wieder! (für sich, Rocco und Leonore betrachtend) Sie sinnen auf und nieder! Könnt' ich versteh'n, was Jeder spricht!

PIZARRO
Nun, Rocco, zög're länger nicht, steig' in den Kerker nieder! (leise) Nicht eher kehrst du wieder, bis ich vollzogen das Gericht!

ROCCO
Nein, Herr, ich zög're länger nicht, ich steige eilend nieder! (für sich) Mir beben meine Glieder; o unglückselig harte Pflicht! (Die Gefangenen gehen in ihre Zellen, die Leonore und Jaquino verschließen.)

MARZELLINE *(watching the prisoners)*
We hasten to behold the light of day—but part again in sorrow. Alas, no cheering ray of joy or hope within these melancholy walls does dwell.

LEONORE *(to the prisoners)*
You hear the word—then linger here no longer. Return into the prison; fear overpowers me! Does no judgment overtake this wicked man?

JAQUINO *(to the prisoners)*
You hear the word—tarry no longer, return into the prison!
(Aside, looking upon Rocco and Leonore) Ah, you are thinking. I wish I knew what you mean to do!

PIZARRO
Now, Rocco, linger no further. Descend into the dungeon! (Softly) Do not return until my will has been accomplished!

ROCCO
No, sir, I tarry no longer, I hasten down. (aside) My limbs tremble; oh severe and dreaded duty!

Act Two

Das Theater stellt einen unterirdischen dunkeln
Kerker vor. Den Zuschauern links ist eine mit
Steinen und Schutt bedeckte Zisterne; im Hinter-
grunde sind mehrere mit Gitterwerk verwahrte
Öffnungen in der Mauer, durch welche man die
Stufen einer von der Höhe herunterführenden
Treppe sieht. Rechts die letzten Stufen und die Tür
in das Gefängniß. Eine Lampe brennt.

The stage shows a dark underground dungeon.
On the left is an old reservoir, covered with stones
and rubbish. In the background are several open-
ings provided with gratings in the wall, through
which a staircase can be seen leading down from
above. Florestan is alone, sitting upon a stone with
a long chain around his waist, fastened to the
wall.

SCENE I

Florestan (allein)
(Er sitzt auf einem Steine, um den Leib hat er eine
lange Kette, deren Ende in der Mauer befestigt ist.)

Florestan (alone)

disc no. 2/track 1

Introduction and Aria The musical introduction to the second act continues the gloom with which the first act ended, as it well should, since it finds
us in Florestan's dungeon cell. The recitative and aria for our hero—the character around whom the entire plot turns—gave Beethoven a great deal of trouble
over the years. It begins as a cry in the dark: "Gott!" (God!) on a sustained high
note for the tenor, and the character's misery and desperation are palpable. He
rationalizes his situation as being part of God's will and eventual justness and
then sings a sadness-tinged aria recounting how he wound up in chains for
telling the truth, but how his consolation is that he has done his duty. Then the
mood changes—Florestan, in some sort of delusionary vision, senses Leonore
coming to free him. His agitation grows and grows until he collapses, both phys-

ically and vocally. In this last section of the aria Beethoven has the tenor singing very high, sustained passages; it is not supposed to sound easy and it never does—the vocal writing is simply too difficult. Beethoven knew it would have just this effect; he wanted it to have an air of desperation about it (while, of course, hoping it would be sung properly). A lonely oboe plays rings around the voice and then the music, like the character, fades off into exhaustion.

FLORESTAN

Gott! welch' Dunkel hier! O grauenvolle Stille! Öd' ist es um mich her: Nichts lebet außer mir. O schwere Prüfung! Doch gerecht ist Gottes Wille! Ich murre nicht: das Maß der Leiden steht bei dir. In des Lebens Frühlingstagen ist das Glück von mir gefloh'n; Wahrheit wagt' ich kühn zu sagen, und die Ketten sind mein Lohn. Willig duld' ich alle Schmerzen, ende schmählich meine Bahn; süßer Trost in meinem Herzen: meine Pflicht hab' ich getan! (in einer an Wahnsinn grenzenden, jedoch ruhigen Begeisterung) Und spür' ich nicht linde, sanft säuselnde Luft? und ist nicht mein Grab mir erhellet? Ich seh', wie ein Engel im rosigen Duft sich tröstend zur Seite mir stellet, – ein Engel, Leonoren, der Gattin so gleich, der führt mich zur Freiheit in's himmlische Reich. (Er sinkt erschöpft von der letzten Gemütsbewegung auf den Felsensitz nieder, seine Hände verhüllen sein Gesicht.)

FLORESTAN

Oh heavens, what dreary gloom! What awful stillness this is. All is desert around, nothing breathes life but me. Oh heavy trial, let the will of god be done. I do not murmur, you know when the cup of sorrow is full. In the days of my spring, happiness—but all happiness has fled. Truth I boldly spoke and chains are my reward; these sufferings I bear willingly and die with resignation; Sweet solace feels thus heart, I fulfilled my duty. (In a state of inspiration, but calmly) Do I not hear soft murmurs in the air? Does not a ray of light surround my grave? Yes, I behold, clad in roseate vapor, a beautiful angel like my Leonore. Stand by my side, to point me out the way to liberty and celestial bliss! (He sinks, exhausted by his last agitation, upon the rocky seat; his hands cover his face.

SCENE II

Rocco, Leonore, Florestan

(Die beiden Ersten, die man bei dem Schein einer Laterne die Treppe herabsteigen sah, tragen einen

Rocco, Leonore, Florestan

Rocco and Leonore, seen through the window by the light of a lantern, carry a pitcher and the tools

Krug und Werkzeuge zum Graben. Die Hintertür öffnet sich und das Theater erhellt sich zur Hälfte.)

for digging. The back door opens and the stage is half-lit.

disc no. 2/track 2 *Melodram und Duett* With Leonore's and Rocco's entry, a melodrama takes place: the two converse in whispered dialogue, underpinned by soft, ominous music. Leonore, close to her goal (and feeling that she will save whomever is imprisoned there), sings a somewhat more florid vocal line in the presence of another person than we've heard her sing before—perhaps because her resolve is stronger, she can expose her true self.

LEONORE
Wie kalt ist es in diesem unterirdischen Gewölbe!

LEONORE
How cold it is, down in this cave.

ROCCO
Das ist natürlich, es ist ja sehr tief.

ROCCO
That's natural, it being so deep.

LEONORE
Ich glaubte schon, wir würden den Eingang gar nicht finden.

LEONORE
I thought we would not find the entrance…

ROCCO
Da ist er.

ROCCO
There he is.

LEONORE
Er scheint ganz ohne Bewegung.

LEONORE
He seems motionless

ROCCO
Vielleicht ist er tot.

ROCCO
Perhaps he is dead.

LEONORE
Tot!?

LEONORE
Dead?!

ROCCO
Nein, nein, er schläft. – Das müssen wir

ROCCO
No, no, he only sleeps. Let's take advantage

benützen und gleich ans Werk gehen. Wir haben keine Zeit zu verlieren.

LEONORE
Es ist unmöglich, seine Züge zu unterscheiden. – Gott, steh mir bei, wenn er es ist!

ROCCO
Hier, unter diesen Trümmern, ist die Zisterne von der ich dir gesagt habe. – Wir brauchen nicht viel zu graben um an die Öffnung zu kommen. Du gib mir eine Haue und stelle dich hierher. – Du zitterst, – fürchtest du dich?

LEONORE
Oh nein, es ist nur so kalt.

ROCCO
So mache fort, beim Arbeiten wird dir schon warm werden.

(Rocco fängt gleich mit dem Ritornell an zu arbeiten. Während dessen benutzt Leonore die Momente, wo sich Rocco bückt, um den Gefangenen zu betrachten.)

ROCCO *(während der Arbeit, mit halblauter Stimme)*
Nur hurtig fort, nur frisch gegraben, es währt nicht lang, er kommt herein.

LEONORE *(ebenfalls arbeitend)*
Ihr sollt ja nicht zu klagen haben, ihr sollt gewiß zufrieden sein.

of that and proceed to work, we have no time to lose.

LEONORE
It is impossible to distinguish his features, but, oh heavens help me if it's him!

ROCCO
Here, below this rubbish is the old cistern, of which I told you. It will not take us long to get at the opening. Give me your pick-axe and come here. You tremble. Are you afraid?

LEONORE
Oh no, it is so cold.

ROCCO
Well then, go on; you will soon get warm with your work.

They begin to dig. During the symphony, Leonore takes advantage of the moment when Rocco stoops to observe the prisoner.

ROCCO *(while at work)*
Only get on quickly, and with smart digging, before long, he will come down.

LEONORE *(also working)*
You shall not have to complain; for to me, no labor is too hard.

ROCCO *(einen großen Stein an der Stelle, wo er hinabstieg, hebend)*
Komm, hilf doch diesen Stein mir heben, – hab Acht! hab Acht! – er hat Gewicht.

LEONORE *(hilft heben)*
Ich helfe schon, – sorgt euch nicht; ich will mir alle Mühe geben.

ROCCO
Ein wenig noch!

LEONORE
Geduld!

ROCCO
Er weicht!

LEONORE
Nur etwas noch!

ROCCO
Es ist nicht leicht!

(Sie rollen den Stein über die Trümmer, und holen Atem.)

ROCCO *(wieder arbeitend)*
Nur hurtig fort u.s.w.

LEONORE *(ebenfalls wieder arbeitend)*
Laßt mich nur wieder Kräfte haben, wir werden bald zu Ende sein.

ROCCO
Nur hurtig fort u.s.w.

ROCCO *(lifting a large stone on the spot where he went down.)*
Come, help me lift this stone. Take care— it is very heavy.

LEONORE
I'll help you directly. Never fear, I'll exert myself to the utmost.

ROCCO
A little more!

LEONORE
Patience!

ROCCO
It moves!

LEONORE
A little more!

ROCCO
It is not light!

They roll the stone over the rubbish and take a breath. Rocco sets to work again.

ROCCO *(working again)*
Hurry—he will be here soon.

LEONORE *(also working again)*
Let me only gain breath again.

ROCCO
He'll be here soon, etc.

LEONORE *(betrachtet den Gefangenen, während Rocco, von ihr abgewendet, mit gekrümmtem Rücken arbeitet; leise, für sich)*
Wer du auch sei'st, ich will dich retten, bei Gott! du sollst kein Opfer sein! Gewiß, ich löse deine Ketten, ich will, du Armer, dich befrei'n.

ROCCO *(sich schnell aufrichtend)*
Was zauderst du in deiner Pflicht?

LEONORE *(fängt wieder an zu arbeiten)*
Mein Vater! nein, ich zaud're nicht.

ROCCO
Nur hurtig fort u.s.w.

LEONORE
Ihr sollt ja nicht u.s.w. Laßt mich nur u.s.w.

(Rocco trinkt; Florestan erholt sich und hebt das Haupt in die Höhe, ohne sich noch gegen Leonore zu wenden.)

disc no. 2/track 3

LEONORE
Er erwacht!

ROCCO
Er erwacht, sagst du?

LEONORE
Ja, er hat soeben seinen Kopf gehoben.

LEONORE *(watching the prisoner, while Rocco turns away)*
Whoever you are, I will save you. By all that's sacred, you shall not fall a sacrifice! For certain, I will loose your chain. I will set you free, you poor wretched man.

ROCCO *(standing up quickly)*
What—are you not working?

LEONORE
No, father, no! I do not hesitate.

ROCCO
He's coming soon, etc.

LEONORE
I will save you, etc.

Rocco takes a drink, Florestan recovers himself and raises his head, without looking at Leonore.

LEONORE
He wakes!

ROCCO
He wakes, you say?

LEONORE
Yes—he has raised his head..

ROCCO
Du bleibst hier! – Ich muß allein mit ihm reden. - Nun, habt ihr ein wenig geruht?

FLORESTAN
Geruht?

LEONORE
(Diese Stimme!)

FLORESTAN
Wie fände ich Ruhe?

LEONORE
(Oh Gott! Er ist's!)

FLORESTAN
Sagt mir, wer ist der Gouverneur dieses Gefängnisses?

ROCCO
Don Pizarro.

FLORESTAN
Pizarro? Schickt nach Sevilla, fragt nach Leonore Florestan...

ROCCO
Ruhe!

FLORESTAN
...sagt ihr, daß ich hier in Ketten liege, sagt ihr ...

ROCCO
Es ist unmöglich, sage ich Euch.

ROCCO
Now have you reposed again a little?

FLORESTAN
How?

LEONORE
(My lord!)

FLORESTAN
How could I rest?

LEONORE
(Oh God! It's him!)

FLORESTAN
Tell me this—who is the governor of this prison?

ROCCO
Don Pizarro.

FLORESTAN
Pizarro? Send to Seville, and ask for Leonore Florestan.

ROCCO
Ach-

FLORESTAN
Tell that I'm lying here in chains

ROCCO
It is impossible, I tell you. I should be ruining myself without helping you.

FLORESTAN
Aus Barmherzigkeit, gebt mir Wasser,
Wasser!

LEONORE
Hier ist etwas Wein.

FLORESTAN
Wer ist das?

ROCCO
Mein Schließer. – Du bist ja so bewegt!

LEONORE
Wer sollte es nicht sein, Ihr selbst, Vater
Rocco ...

ROCCO
Du hast recht. Der Mensch hat so eine
Stimme ...

LEONORE
Ja, sie dringt in die Tiefe des Herzens.

FLORESTAN
At least, get me a glass of water!

LEONORE
Here it is, drink.

FLORESTAN
Who is that?

ROCCO
It is true, the man has such a voice!

LEONORE
Who could be helping? You, yourself,
Father Rocco ...

ROCCO
It's true, the lad has such a voice ...

LEONORE
It penetrates me to the depths of my heart.

disc no. 2/track 4   *Terzetto* In this terzetto, at one point Leonore gives Florestan bread and he thanks her for her kindness. Has music ever expressed gentleness more eloquently?

FLORESTAN
Euch werde Lohn in bessern Welten, der
Himmel hat euch mir geschickt. O Dank!
Ihr habt mich süß erquickt; ich kann die
Wohltat nicht vergelten.

FLORESTAN
May you find a reward in the next world.
Heaven has sent you to me. Oh, thanks!
You have sweetly revived me. I cannot
reward thy kindness.

ROCCO *(leise zu Leonore, die er bei Seite zieht)*
Ich labt' ihn gern, den armen Mann, es ist
ja bald um ihn getan.

LEONORE *(für sich)*
Wie heftig pocht dieses Herz, es wogt in
Freud' und scharfem Schmerz!

FLORESTAN *(für sich)*
Bewegt seh' ich den Jüngling hier,
und Rührung zeigt auch dieser Mann. O
Gott, du sendest Hoffnung mir, daß ich sie
noch gewinnen kann.

LEONORE
Die hehre, bange Stunde winkt, die Tod
mir oder Rettung bringt.

ROCCO
Ich tu', was meine Pflicht gebeut, doch
hass' ich alle Grausamkeit.

LEONORE *(leise zu Rocco, indem sie ein
Stückchen Brot aus der Tasche zieht)*
Dies Stückchen Brot, – ja, seit zwei Tagen
trag' ich es immer schon bei mir.

ROCCO
Ich möchte gern, doch sag' ich dir, das
hieße wirklich zu viel wagen.

LEONORE
Ach! (schmeichelnd) Ihr labtet gern den
armen Mann.

ROCCO *(Softly, to Leonore)*
I was glad, Heaven knows, to refresh to
poor man. But, it is already over with him.
I do what my duty imposes, but I abhor
cruelty.

LEONORE *(aside)*
How my heart is beating; my life fluctuates
between joy and grief.

FLORESTAN *(to himself)*
I see this youth here affected and this man
also shows compassion. Oh God! You send
me hope, that I may again find her for
whom alone I live.

LEONORE
The awful hour beckons on, that death or
deliverance does bring!

ROCCO
I do what my duty imposes, yet I abhor
this cruelty.

LEONORE *(Softly to Rocco, while she draws a
small piece of bread out of her pocket.)*
This piece of bread I have carried about me
for the last two days.

ROCCO
I would give it to him willingly, but I
would be venturing too much.

LEONORE
Ah! You must help this poor man.

ROCCO
Das geht nicht an, das geht nicht an.

LEONORE *(wie vorhin)*
Es ist ja bald um ihn getan.

ROCCO
So sei es, ja, so sei's! du kannst es wagen.

LEONORE *(in größter Bewegung Florestan
das Brot reichend)*
Da nimm das Brot, du armer Mann!

FLORESTAN *(Leonorens Hand ergreifend und an
sich drückend)*
O dank dir, Dank, o Dank! Euch werde
Lohn in bessern Welten, der Himmel hat
euch mir geschickt. O Dank, ihr habt mich
süß erquickt! Bewegt seh' ich den Jüngling
hier, und Rührung zeigt auch dieser Mann,
o wenn ich sie gewinnen kann!

LEONORE
Der Himmel schicke Rettung dir, dann
wird mir hoher Lohn gewährt. Ihr labt' ihn
gern, den armen Mann!

ROCCO
Mich rührte oft dein Leiden hier, doch
Hilfe war mir streng verwehrt. (für sich)
Ich labt' ihn gern, den armen Mann, es ist
ja bald um ihn getan!

LEONORE
O mehr, als ich ertragen kann!

ROCCO
That will not do, it will not do.

LEONORE *(as before)*
It will all soon be over for him.

ROCCO
So be it then, you may venture it.

LEONORE *(in great agitation, she hands Florestan
the bread.)*
There, take this bread, poor man!

FLORESTAN *(grasping Leonore's hand and pressing
it to himself)*
Thank you, thank you!
May you find a reward in the next world.
Heaven has sent you to me. Oh, thanks!
You have sweetly revived me. I cannot
reward your kindness. I wish that I could
reward you!

LEONORE
Heaven send you deliverance—then will I
be rewarded.

ROCCO
Your sufferings often moved me, but to
keep you was strictly forbidden to me.

LEONORE
Oh, this is more than I can endure!

FLORESTAN
O daß ich euch nicht lohnen kann!   (Florestan verschlingt das Stück Brot.)

FLORESTAN
I wish I could reward you!
(Florestan eats the piece of bread.)

disc no. 2/track 5

ROCCO *(nach augenblicklichem Stillschweigen)*
Alles ist bereit. Ich gehe das Signal zu geben.

ROCCO *(after a moment)*
All is ready. I am going to give the signal

FLORESTAN
Wo geht er hin? (Pfiff) Ist das der Vorbote meines Todes?

FLORESTAN
Where are you going?
Is that the harbinger of death?

LEONORE
Beruhige dich! Vergiß nicht, es gibt eine Vorsehung. Ja! Es gibt eine Vorsehung.

LEONORE
Be composed—do not forget that there is a Providence above.

(Sie entfernt sich und geht gegen die Zisterne.)

(She separates from him, and goes toward the cistern.)

SCENE III

Vorige, Pizarro (vermummt in einen Mantel)

The former, Pizarro (disguised)

PIZARRO *(zu Rocco, die Stimme verstellend)*
Ist alles bereit?

PIZARRO *(To Rocco, in a fake voice)*
Is everything ready?

ROCCO
Ja, Herr! – Soll ich ihm die Ketten abnehmen?

ROCCO
Yes, sir!! – Must I not take the irons from the prisoner?

PIZARRO
Nein! Schließ ihn nur los. Die Zeit drängt.

PIZARRO
No! I must rid myself of these two.

Quartet This quartet, beginning with Pizarro's pronouncement, "Er sterbe!" (He shall die!), is an amazing five minutes of music. Its beginning is cruel and sinister, and the tension and passions of the individuals keep swelling until they are finally interrupted by Leonore's shocking declaration, "Tot erst sein Weib" (First kill his wife!) on its high, fortissimo B-flat. This, in turn, leads immediately away from all previously experienced emotions into a new, total confusion, as the characters discover what we've known all along. Everything comes to a momentary halt with Leonore drawing a pistol and a trumpeter announcing the arrival of the Minister (and salvation) but then continues at once growing in intensity to a near hysterical end. It is a musical scene so well constructed that, despite its frenzy, every voice can be heard and every emotion is clear.

PIZARRO
Er sterbe! Doch er soll erst wissen, wer ihm sein stolzes Herz zerfleischt. Der Rache Dunkel sei zerrissen! Sieh' her, du hast mich nicht getäuscht! (Er schlägt den Mantel auf.) Pizarro, den du stürzen wolltest, Pizarro, den du fürchten solltest, steht nun als Rächer hier.

FLORESTAN (gefaßt)
Ein Mörder steht vor mir.

PIZARRO
Noch einmal ruf' ich dir, was du getan, zurück. Nur noch ein Augenblick, und dieser Dolch – (Er will Florestan durchbohren.)

LEONORE (stürzt mit einem durchdringenden Geschrei hervor und bedeckt Florestan mit ihrem Leibe)
Zurück!

PIZARRO
He dies; but he shall first know who it is that pierces his proud heart. Let the darkness be torn away that veils revenge. Behold! You have not deceived yourself! (He throws off his disguise.) Pizarro, whom you wished to overthrow! Pizarro, whom you should be afraid to look at, stands now before you, his own avenger!

FLORESTAN (calmly)
A murderer stands before me.

PIZARRO
Yet, for once will I recall you to what you have don; yet one moment and my dagger— (He lunges at Florestan.)

LEONORE (springs forward with a scream, blocking Florestan)
Stop!

FLORESTAN
O Gott!

ROCCO
Was soll?

LEONORE
Durchbohren mußt du erst diese Brust!
Der Tod sei dir geschworen für deine
Mörderlust.

PIZARRO *(schleudert sie fort)*
Wahnsinniger!

ROCCO *(zu Leonore)*
Halt' ein! halt' ein!

FLORESTAN
O Gott! o mein Gott!

PIZARRO
Er soll bestrafet sein!

LEONORE *(noch einmal ihren Mann bedeckend)*
Töt' erst sein Weib!

PIZARRO
Sein Weib?

ROCCO
Sein Weib?

FLORESTAN
Mein Weib?

LEONORE *(zu Florestan)*
Ja, sieh' hier Leonore!

FLORESTAN
O God!

ROCCO
What's this?

LEONORE
You must stab through this breast. Death is
sworn to you for your blood-thirstiness!

PIZARRO *(thrusting her away)*
Mad creature!

ROCCO *(to Leonore)*
Stop!

FLORESTAN
Oh God! My God!

PIZARRO
He shall be punished!

LEONORE *(once more shielding her husband)*
Kill first his wife!

PIZARRO
His wife?

ROCCO
His wife?

FLORESTAN
My wife?

LEONORE *(to Florestan)*
Yes, it's me, your Leonore!

FLORESTAN
Leonore!

LEONORE *(zu den Anderen)*
Ich bin sein Weib, geschworen
hab' ich ihm Trost, Verderben dir!

PIZARRO *(für sich)*
Welch' unerhörter Mut!

FLORESTAN *(zu Leonore)*
Vor Freude starrt mein Blut!

ROCCO
Mir starrt vor Angst mein Blut!

LEONORE *(für sich)*
Ich trotze seiner Wut!

PIZARRO
Soll ich vor einem Weibe beben?

LEONORE
Der Tod sei dir geschworen!

PIZARRO
So opfr' ich beide meinem Grimm.
(Dringt wieder auf sie und Florestan ein.)

LEONORE
Durchbohren mußt du erst diese Brust!

PIZARRO
Geteilt hast du mit ihm das Leben, so teile
nun den Tod mit ihm!

FLORESTAN
Leonore!

LEONORE *(to the others)*
I am his wife. I have sworn aid to him,
destruction to you!

PIZARRO *(aside)*
What courage!

FLORESTAN *(to Leonore)*
My heart will burst with joy!

ROCCO
My blood runs cold with terror!

LEONORE *(aside)*
I brave his rage!

PIZARRO
Shall I tremble before a woman?

LEONORE
I promise, death to you!

PIZARRO
No! I will sacrifice them both to my rage.

LEONORE
I do not fear you- I have sworn revenge!

PIZARRO
You have shared life with him, now share
death.

LEONORE *(zieht hastig eine kleine Pistole aus der Brust und hält sie Pizarro vor)*
Noch einen Laut – und du bist tot!
(Leonore hängt an Florestans Halse.)
Ach! du bist gerettet! großer Gott!

FLORESTAN
Ach! ich bin gerettet! großer Gott!

PIZARRO (BETÄUBT)
Ha! der Minister! Höll' und Tod!

ROCCO *(betäubt)*
O was ist das? gerechter Gott!

(Pizarro steht betäubt; eben so Rocco. Leonore hängt an Florestan's Halse. Man hört die Trompete stärker. Pause.)

LEONORE *(drawing a pistol out of her bosom and holds it before Pizarro)*
Another word, and you are dead.
(Lenore hangs on Florestan's neck.)
Oh! The heavens! Good God!

FLORESTAN
Oh! Merciful God!

PIZARRO
Ha! The minister! Hell and death!

ROCCO
What is this? Heavenly God!

(Pizarro stands confounded. Rocco, the same. The trumpet sounds louder.)

SCENE IV

Vorige, Jaquino, zwei Offiziere, Soldaten (mit Fackeln) (Jaquino, Offiziere und Soldaten erscheinen an der obersten Gitteröffnung der Treppe.)

JAQUINO *(spricht während der Musikpause)*
Vater Rocco! Vater Rocco! Der Herr Minister ist angekommen!

ROCCO
Gelobt sei Gott! Wir kommen, ja wir kommen augenblicklich! Und Leute mit Fackeln sollen heruntersteigen und den Gouverneur hinaufbegleiten!

The former, Jaquino, two Officers, Soldiers (with torches)

JAQUINO *(speaking while the music pauses)*
Father Rocco! The Minister arrives; his guard is already at the castle gate!

ROCCO
Heaven be praised! We are coming, yes, we're coming immediately; and the men with their torches shall come down and accompany the Governor up.

(Die Soldaten kommen bis an die Tür herunter. Die Offiziere und Jaquino gehen oben ab.)

LEONORE UND FLORESTAN
Es schlägt der Rache Stunde, du sollst/ich soll gerettet sein! Die Liebe wird im Bunde mit Mute dich/mich befrei'n!

PIZARRO
Verflucht sei diese Stunde! die Heuchler spotten mein! Verzweiflung wird im Bunde mit meiner Rache sein!

ROCCO
O fürchterliche Stunde! O Gott! was wartet mein? Ich will nicht mehr im Bunde mit diesem Wütrich sein! *(Pizarro stürzt fort, indem er Rocco einen Wink gibt, ihm zu folgen; dieser benützt den Augenblick, da Pizarro schon geht, faßt die Hände beider Gatten, drückt sie an seine Brust, deutet gen Himmel und eilt nach. Die Soldaten leuchten Pizarro voraus.)*

SCENE V

Leonore, Florestan

FLORESTAN
Leonore!

LEONORE
Florestan!

(The soldiers come down as far as the door. The Officers and Jaquino go out again.)

LEONORE AND FLORESTAN
The moment of vengeance has come; you shall be free! Love, in league with courage, will make us free.

PIZARRO
Cursed be this hour! Hell mocks me! Despair now leagues itself with my revenge!

ROCCO
Dread suspense! Oh, what fresh affliction is now in store for me? I will no longer be controlled by this tyrant. The moment of vengeance has come; you shall be free. *(Pizarro hurries away, giving Rocco a sign to follow him. He avails himself of the moment when Pizarro is going and unites the hands of the husband and wife, presses them to his chest, points to heaven and follows him.)*

Leonore, Florestan

FLORESTAN
Leonore!

LEONORE
Florestan!

Duet The couple's ecstatic duet, "O namenlose Freude!" (O nameless joy) is just that: its high-lying, florid vocal line is overlapping, anxious, euphoric. The joy that they feel runs so deep that there's an element of hysteria to it: they've been grief-stricken for so long that when their repressed feelings finally erupt, what we hear is nothing short of sheer rapture.

LEONORE UND FLORESTAN
O namenlose Freude! Mein Mann an meiner Brust!/An Leonorens Brust! Nach unnennbaren Leiden so übergroße Lust!

LEONORE
Du wieder nun in meinen Armen!

FLORESTAN
O Gott! wie groß ist dein Erbarmen!

LEONORE UND FLORESTAN
O dank dir, Gott, für diese Lust!
Mein Mann/Weib an meiner Brust!

SCENE VI

Rocco, die Vorigen
(Rocco stürzt herein. Alle drei ab.)

VERWANDLUNG
Paradeplatz des Schlosses, mit der Statue des Königs.

SCENE VII

DON FERNANDO, PIZARRO, JAQUINO, MARZELLINE,
Offiziere, Schloßwachen, die Gefangenen,

LEONORE AND FLORESTAN
Oh, nameless joy, to be at my [husbands/Leonore's] breast after great suffering.

LEONORE
To have you in my arms!

FLORESTAN
Oh God, delight and joy!

LEONORE UND FLORESTAN
Oh thank you, great God, that we are here together. Etc.

Rocco, the former
(Rocco springs in.)

EVERYONE
Everyone up to see the minister! Let us all be freed!

DON FERNANDO, PIZARRO, JAQUINO, MARZELLINE,
Officers, Guards, Don Fernando

Volk
(Die Schloßwachen marschieren auf und
bilden ein offenes Viereck. Dann erscheint
von einer Seite der Minister Don Fernando, von Pizarro und Offizieren begleitet.
Volk eilt herzu. Von der andern Seite
treten, von Jaquino und Marzelline
geführt, die Staatsgefangenen ein, die vor
Don Fernando niederknieen.

(The castle guard march up, then the minister don Fernando, accompanied by
Pizarro and Officers. People assemble as
spectators, and the prisoners appear with
Jaquino and Marzelline. They all throw
themselves on their knees before Don Fernando.)

disc no. 2/
tracks 8 & 9

Finale Beethoven instructed that no more than seven seconds should
elapse between the end of the duet and the start of the finale. He wanted the
hero's and heroine's joy to give way to general rejoicing at once, and it does.
The chorus greets the minister, Don Fernando, happily; he, in turn, is overjoyed
to see his old friend Florestan, and the fates of all the characters are changed in
five glorious minutes. Our hero and heroine sing of their wonder together slowly,
almost trancelike (with a sympathetic solo oboe), while the others raise their
voices piously, peacefully to God (although Marzelline's vocal line expresses a
very genuine and sad confusion).

DAS VOLK UND DIE GEFANGENEN
Heil! Heil sei dem Tag, Heil sei der Stunde,
die lang ersehnt, doch unvermeint,
Gerechtigkeit mit Huld im Bunde,
vor unsers Grabes Tor erscheint! Heil!

CHORUS
All hail the day! All hail the hour, long
sought for yet unhoped! Justice, united
with mercy, appears to us on the shrine of
death.

DON FERNANDO
Des besten Königs Wink und Wille führt
mich zu euch, ihr Armen, her, daß ich der
Frevel Nacht enthülle, die All' umfangen
schwarz und schwer. Nicht länger knieet
sklavisch nieder, (Die Gefangenen stehen
auf.) Tyrannenstrenge sei mir fern. Es sucht
der Bruder seine Brüder, und kann er
helfen, hilft er gern.

DON FERNANDO
The command and wish of the best of
kings brings me to you, poor wearied suf-
ferers! That I unveil crimes and dreary sor-
rows, which surround you deep and full.
No longer kneel down slavishly.

DAS VOLK UND DIE GEFANGENEN
Heil sei dem Tag! Heil sei der Stunde! Heil!

DON FERNANDO
Es sucht der Bruder u.s.w.

CHORUS
All hail the day!

DON FERNANDO
I come a brother loving and help where I can, etc.

SCENE VIII

*Die Vorigen, Rocco (durch die Wachen dringend),
hinter ihm Leonore und Florestan*

*The former, Rocco, bring in Leonore and Florestan
with him*

ROCCO
Wohlan, so helfet! helft den Armen!

ROCCO
There, there! Help here, help the poor captive!

PIZARRO
Was seh' ich? Ha!

PIZARRO
What is this? Ha!

ROCCO *(zu Pizarro)*
Bewegt es dich?

ROCCO *(to Pizarro)*
Does it move you?

PIZARRO *(zu Rocco)*
Fort, fort!

PIZARRO *(to Rocco)*
Away, away!

DON FERNANDO *(zu Rocco)*
Nun rede!

DON FERNANDO *(to Rocco)*
No, speak!

ROCCO
All' Erbarmen
vereine diesem Paare sich!
(Florestan vorführend)
Don Florestan –

ROCCO
For mercy's sake, have pity and reunite this hapless pair.
(Florestan advances)
Don Florestan –

DON FERNANDO *(staunend)*
Der Totgeglaubte,
der Edle, der für Wahrheit stritt?

ROCCO
Und Qualen ohne Zahl erlitt.

DON FERNANDO
Mein Freund, der Totgeglaubte? –
Gefesselt, bleich steht er vor mir.

LEONORE UND ROCCO
Ja, Florestan, ihr seht ihn hier.

ROCCO *(Leonore vorstellend)*
Und Leonore –

DON FERNANDO *(noch mehr betroffen)*
Leonore?

ROCCO
Der Frauen Zierde führ' ich vor,
sie kam hierher –

PIZARRO
Zwei Worte sagen –

DON FERNANDO
Kein Wort! (zu Rocco)
Sie kam? –

ROCCO
Dort an mein Tor, und trat als
Knecht in meine Dienste, und tat so

DON FERNANDO *(stunned)*
He that was supposed dead? The hero, who
fought for truth and right?

ROCCO
And who has suffered unimaginable
torment.

DON FERNANDO
My friend, supposed dead! How is this,
that chained, pallid and exhausted, he
stands before me?

LEONORE AND ROCCO
Yes, Florestan, you see him here.

ROCCO *(presenting her)*
And Leonore –

DON FERNANDO *(still more affected)*
Leonore?

ROCCO
She is the pride of her sex, she came here…

PIZARRO
Speak but two words –

DON FERNANDO
Not a word!
(to Rocco) She came?

ROCCO
There, at my gate—she entered my service
as a hireling boy, and served me so well and

brave treue Dienste, daß ich – zum Eidam
sie erkor.

MARZELLINE
O weh' mir! was vernimmt mein Ohr!

ROCCO
Der Unmensch wollt' in dieser Stunde vollzieh'n an Florestan den Mord –

PIZARRO (in größter Wut)
Vollzieh'n! Mit ihm! –

ROCCO (auf sich und Leonoren deutend)
Mit uns im Bunde! (zu Don Fernando)
Nur euer Kommen rief ihn fort.

DAS VOLK UND DIE GEFANGENEN (sehr lebhaft)
Bestrafet sei der Bösewicht, der Unschuld
unterdrückt! Gerechtigkeit hält zum
Gericht der Rache Schwert gezückt.
(Pizarro wird abgeführt.)

DON FERNANDO (zu Rocco)
Du schlossest auf des Edlen Grab, jetzt
nimm ihm seine Ketten ab! Doch halt! –
Euch, edle Frau, allein, euch ziemt es ganz
ihn zu befrei'n.

LEONORE (nimmt die Schlüssel, löst, in größter
Bewegung, Florestan die Ketten ab; er sinkt in
Leonorens Arme)
O Gott! welch' ein Augenblick!

FLORESTAN
O unaussprechlich süßes Glück!

MARZELLINE
Oh woe is me! What do I hear?

ROCCO
Within this very hour, the cruel man
would do a deed of murder to Florestan.

PIZARRO
Murder? To him?

ROCCO (pointing to himself and Leonore)
Yes, my lord, he wanted us to join in his
base plan. Your arrival drove him away.

CHORUS
Punishment be to the villain who
oppressed the innocent! Justice for judgment, the drawn sword of revenge.

DON FERNANDO (to Rocco)
You lifted the grave that threatened this
noble hears—now take off his chains—yet
stay—You noble woman! To you alone it
becomes completely to set him free.

LEONORE (takes the keys, loosens the chains from
Florestan, He sinks into her arms)
Oh! What a moment!

FLORESTAN
Oh inexpressible joy!

DON FERNANDO
Gerecht, o Gott, ist dein Gericht!

MARZELLINE UND ROCCO
Du prüfest, du verläßt uns nicht.

ALLE
O Gott! o welch' ein Augenblick u.s.w.

disc no. 2/track 10

DAS VOLK UND DIE GEFANGENEN
Wer ein holdes Weib errungen,
stimm' in unsern Jubel ein!
Nie wird es zu hoch besungen,
Retterin des Gatten sein.

FLORESTAN
Deine Treu' erhielt mein Leben,
Tugend schreckt den Bösewicht.

LEONORE
Liebe führte mein Bestreben,
wahre Liebe fürchtet nicht.

DAS VOLK UND DIE GEFANGENEN
Preist mit hoher Freude Glut
Leonorens edlen Mut!

FLORESTAN (*vortretend und auf Leonore weisend*)
und die Männer Wer ein solches Weib u.s.w.

LEONORE (*ihn umarmend*)
Liebend ist es mir gelungen, dich aus Ket-

DON FERNANDO
Just, Oh heaven, are your judgments!

MARZELLINE AND ROCCO
You tried—but you did not forsake us.

ALL
Oh! What a moment, what joy, etc.

CHORUS
Whoever has obtained such a partner of his heart, let him join in our celebration. Who can ever praise the wife enough, who frees her husband from his chains.

FLORESTAN
Your fidelity restores my life. Virtue is the sinner's dread!

LEONORE
Love guided my endeavors, true love knows no fear.

CHORUS
Let us sing praises high to the noble strife of Leonore.

FLORESTAN (*advancing, pointing to Leonore*)
Whoever has obtained a wife, etc.

LEONORE (*embracing him*)
Guided by love, my success is complete.

ten zu befrei'n; liebend sei es hoch besungen, Florestan ist wieder mein!

MARZELLINE, JAQUINO, DON FERNANDO UND ROCCO
Wer ein solches Weib u.s.w.

Ende

Your chains are broken! High praise is to love; I embrace my Florestan again.

ALL
Whoever has a wife, etc.

End

PHOTO CREDITS

Fidelio

OPERA IN TWO ACTS

COMPACT DISC ONE 69:28:00

COMPACT DISC TWO   45.21

Act Two